STUDENT UNIT GUIDE

NEW EDITION

Edexcel AS Psychology Unit 1
Social and Cognitive Psychology

Christine Brain

PHILIP ALLAN

Philip Allan Updates, an imprint of Hodder Education, an Hachette UK company, Market Place, Deddington, Oxfordshire OX15 0SE

Orders

Bookpoint Ltd, 130 Milton Park, Abingdon, Oxfordshire OX14 4SB
tel: 01235 827827
fax: 01235 400401
e-mail: education@bookpoint.co.uk
Lines are open 9.00 a.m.–5.00 p.m., Monday to Saturday, with a 24-hour message answering service.
You can also order through the Philip Allan Updates website: www.philipallan.co.uk

ISBN 978-1-4441-6284-4

First printed 2012
Impression number 5 4 3 2
Year 2017 2016 2015 2014 2013

Typeset by Integra, India

Printed in Dubai

Hachette UK's policy is to use papers that are natural, renewable and recyclable products and made from wood grown in sustainable forests. The logging and manufacturing processes are expected to conform to the environmental regulations of the country of origin.

Contents

Content Guidance

Questions & Answers

Getting the most from this book

Questions & Answers

Exam-style questions

Examiner comments on the questions

Tips on what you need to do to gain full marks, indicated by the icon **e**.

Sample student answers

Practise the questions, then look at the student answers that follow each set of questions.

Examiner commentary on sample student answers

Find out how many marks each answer would be awarded in the exam and then read the examiner comments (preceded by the icon **e**) following each student answer. Some comments include annotations that link back to points made in the student answers, to show exactly how and where marks are gained or lost.

About this book

This is a guide to Unit 1 of the Edexcel AS Psychology specification. Before looking at what this guide is all about, here is some good news. You can pass the exam for this unit and you can do well. How can I draw this conclusion without knowing you? Because you are reading this guide.

However, this guide:
- is not a textbook — there is no substitute for reading the required material and taking notes
- does not tell you the actual questions on your paper or give you the answers

Aims

The aim of this guide is to provide you with a clear understanding of the requirements of Unit 1 of the AS specification and to advise you on how best to meet these requirements.

This guide looks at:
- the psychology you need to know about
- what you need to be able to do and what skills you need
- how you could go about learning the necessary material
- what is being examined
- what you should expect in the examination
- how you could tackle the different styles of exam question
- the format of the exam, including what questions might look like
- how questions are marked, including examples of answers, with examiner's comments

How to use this guide

A good way of using this guide is to read it through in the order in which it is presented. Alternatively, you can consider each topic in the Content Guidance section, and then turn to a relevant question in the Questions & Answers section. Whichever way you use the guide, try some of the questions yourself to test your learning. If you are working with someone else, mark each other's answers. Working with someone else is more enjoyable and means you are actively learning. For example, try explaining the material to others, as this is an effective way of learning. Have your textbooks available too — you will need access to all the relevant information.

If you need to, draw up a revision plan now, remind yourself that you want to succeed and practise some relaxation techniques.

How to learn the material

- Make notes, be concise and use your own notes for final revision.
- Have a separate sheet of paper for each approach.

- For each approach, note down the six headings (see the summary at the start of each approach) and use these as a guide. Leave room to fit your notes in under each heading.
- Read through each section, then make brief notes as needed.
- Be sure to make notes on evaluation points.
- Finally, note down briefly three descriptive aspects of a key issue and six 'facts' linking concepts to the issue.

Another useful method is to use cards for each topic. Have the topic heading on one side of the card and brief notes on the other. Remember to note down equal amounts of knowledge and evaluation.

Glossary

A list of terms is included at the end of this guide (pages 92–100). They are organised alphabetically and subdivided into each approach — the social approach and the cognitive approach. This is a list of definitions that can help you in your revision. If you are working with a friend, for example, test each other by asking for the definition of ten terms each, alternating and then reading out the term and checking the definition.

The glossary can also be used to draw up revision cards. Write the term on one side and your own definition (formed by putting it into your own words) on the other side.

You could also go through the glossary matching terms to approaches, which will help your learning, picking out all the methodology terms to draw them together.

Think of other ways of using the glossary. For example, you could write out some definitions in your own words and, a few days later, identify the term being defined.

Examination issues

You need to know that there are two approaches to cover for Unit 1 and within each approach there are six sections: definitions, methodology, content, studies in detail, key issue and practical. This structure is reflected in the content sections that follow.

Also note that there are three assessment objectives (AOs):
- AO1, which is about knowledge with understanding
- AO2, which is about comment and evaluation
- AO3, which covers the 'science' part of the unit — 'doing psychology'

A good plan is to consider the exam paper as covering the three AOs in equal proportions (one third each) and to consider the two approaches to be evenly covered. That will help you when preparing.

Content Guidance

The social approach

Unit 1 covers the social and the cognitive approaches. This section looks at the social approach. For some areas of Unit 1 you can choose what you study. In this section suitable material is presented, but you may have studied different examples. *You might be better advised to revise the material you chose for your course. However, you can choose what is summarised in the box below.*

Table 1 Summary of the social approach

Definition and key terms
The approach is defined in this section, and key terms are listed and briefly explained. The key terms are defined where they appear in the Content Guidance section.
Methodology
The survey method, including questionnaires and interviews, is outlined, together with an evaluation. Qualitative and quantitative data, both used in surveys, are outlined as well, again with evaluation. Four sampling techniques are covered, as are five ethical issues in 'doing' psychology.
Content
Obedience is defined and agency theory — which is a way of understanding obedience — is explained. Milgram's (a main figure in the field of obedience) main study and variations are outlined (you need to know one), with evaluation and consideration of ethics. Meeus and Raijmakers's study (a study of obedience in another country) is outlined and evaluated too and comparisons are made to consider cultural differences. The social identity theory of prejudice is explained, with definitions of prejudice and discrimination.
Two studies in detail
Hofling et al. (1966) and Reicher and Haslam (2003/6) are described and evaluated. You may have studied Tajfel's work or Sherif's study instead.
Key issue
The issue of blind obedience in a prison setting (Abu Ghraib) is covered, but you may have looked at one or more different key issues.
Practical
You will have carried out at least one practical within social psychology and you should use your own practical, because you will have 'learned by doing'. Some ideas about the practical are suggested in this book.

Definition and key terms

The social approach is about people, both as individuals and as part of a group or groups. It is about how people live together comfortably, and when they do not, as well as about social structures — who obeys, who gives orders. Questions considered

Knowledge check 1

Define social psychology, including two examples.

Knowledge check 2

Define each key term and provide one example each time.

in social psychology include why people obey, why people help or do not help others, why people are attracted to certain people, and why some people are aggressive, for example in crowds.

Key terms you need to know: agentic state, autonomous state, moral strain, in-group, out-group, social categorisation, social identification, social comparison. These are dealt with in the Content section later on (see page 19).

Summary

Social approach — definition and key terms

- The social approach involves studying how people interact with one another, including issues like hostility towards other individuals and obeying those in authority.
- The social approach can also compare cultures to examine group and individual behaviour patterns.

- Key terms/concepts in the area of obedience include the agentic and autonomous state, and moral strain.
- Key terms/concepts in the area of prejudice include in-group/out-group and three concepts within the social identity theory: social categorisation, social identification and social comparison.

Examiner tip

In the examination, 'definition' questions are often found, usually for 2 or 3 marks. You can get 1 mark for a basic definition, 2 marks if you explain in some detail, and for a third mark it is a good idea to add an example that illustrates the term or concept clearly.

Methodology

Why methodology is important

Methodology concerns how psychology is carried out — the main point being to ensure that findings (results and conclusions) are secure. 'Secure' involves various issues that are evaluation points, such as **validity**, **reliability**, **generalisability**, **objectivity**, **credibility** — and there are other important evaluation issues, such as ethical issues. To get 'secure' data, the methodology of a study is carefully planned. This is what the methodology sections in your course are about. Methodology is the study of the way a study is carried out.

Table 2 Key methodology evaluation terms

Methodology evaluation term	Explanation
Validity	Measuring what you claim to measure, meaning that what you measure is 'real life' and not something forced because of the study's methodology.
Reliability	Getting the same results if you do a study again, because if you do not get the same results, the data are not worth much. To test for reliability there needs to be replicability (the study has to be capable of being repeated).
Generalisability	The sampling is such that results can be said to be true of other people that the study is meant to represent.
Objectivity/subjectivity	The study is not biased because of the researcher giving their own opinions or influencing the results. Controls, for example, help to keep a study objective. Subjectivity is what occurs when the researcher affects the results with their own views.
Credibility	When the findings (results and conclusions) of a study are explained, people accept them. The data seem believable (credible). The methodology is also sound.

Knowledge check 3

For each term in the table, choose another term and make two comparison points.

Basic methodological features of a study

A study will have an **aim** and most studies will have a **hypothesis**. There are **variables**, and for most studies there will be an **independent variable (IV)** and a **dependent variable (DV)**, both of which have to be carefully **operationalised**. Generally, there are **controls** over other variables, such as **situational variables** and **participant variables**. These are key methodology description terms.

Table 3 Key methodology description terms

Methodology description term	Explanation
Aim	A brief statement of what the study is intending to find, such as 'to see if people are more hostile to someone who is not a member of their own group'.
Hypothesis (alternative)	A carefully defined statement of what the study is aiming to find. The IV and the DV are both clearly stated, saying exactly what is being done and what is being measured. The social approach talks about the alternative hypothesis, which is the overall term for the statement. (Then there is an experimental hypothesis — for experiments — and a null hypothesis, explained later.)
Operationalising	Making something measurable and clear. For example, to study the aim given here, hostility has to be measured somehow, as does what the in-group and the out-group are. This is done by operationalising the variables — making them measurable.
Independent variable (IV)	The variable that the researcher manipulates (changes) to see the effect on the dependent variable. For example, a study could look at whether two people act differently depending on whether they belong to the same group or to two different groups. The IV is whether they belong to the same group (in-group) or to two different groups (out-group).
Conditions	An IV has more than one condition, as it is about the different way that X or Y would affect the DV. There are often two conditions, such as in the example used here, where one condition is the in-group (people in your group) and the other is the out-group (people not in your group).
Dependent variable (DV)	The variable that is measured to see the effect of the IV. In the example about in-group/out-group behaviour the DV was 'act differently', and that would have to be operationalised. For example, saying nice things about the in-group members and unpleasant things about the out-group members, as measured by questionnaire.
Control	The IV is changed and the DV measured, but everything else is controlled to make sure nothing else affects the results. For example, making sure that not all the in-group are female and the out-group male, otherwise you might find hostility to the out-group because of gender differences, not because they are 'out-group'. Controls are put in place to keep everything the same except for the IV/DV.

Methodology description term	Explanation
Situational variables	Variables in the situation such as noise, temperature and light might affect the results if they are different in the different conditions.
Participant variables	Variables in the participants such as mood, hunger, age or gender might affect the results if they are different in the different conditions.

Research methods

Methodology is all about the methods used in psychology to gather data. Research methods you will cover include surveys, which comprise questionnaires and interviews; experiments, which include field, laboratory and natural experiments; case studies and observations. Each approach focuses on different research methods (as well as different aspects of methodology).

Table 4 Approaches (Unit 1 and Unit 2) and related research method

Approach	Main research method focused on
Social	Survey (questionnaires and interviews)
Cognitive	Experiments (laboratory, field and natural)
Psychodynamic	Case studies (including Freud's style of case study)
Biological	General testing
Learning	Observations

Questionnaires

Questionnaires gather **personal data** because the researcher needs to know something about the respondent (the person answering). But only necessary data should be gathered. For example, if you do not need to know someone's job, do not ask.

Then there are questions that extract the other data required. For example, if the aim is to see if people are more hostile to someone who is not a member of their own group, the questionnaire needs to find out about people's attitudes to people in groups to which they belong and people in other groups.

There are many different ways of asking such questions, such as using a **Likert-type scale** (strongly agree, agree, don't know, disagree, strongly disagree) or any other rating scale. Questions can simply ask for 'yes' or 'no' answers. Other questions can ask directly for someone's opinion, such as 'What do you think about...?'

Closed questions

Closed questions are those where the answer is a forced choice — the respondent has no chance of giving any answer other than the choice given. An example of a closed question (sometimes called a closed-ended question) is a question asking for the answer 'yes' or 'no'.

Table 5 Strengths and weaknesses of closed-ended questions

Strengths	Weaknesses
Generate standard replies that can be counted for ease of comparability and analysis	Force a choice of answer (even 'unsure') so may not give the answer respondents would prefer, so they are not valid
Same clearly expressed, detailed questions, so if repeated tend to get the same responses; reliable	'Unsure' can mean 'don't know' or 'sometimes yes and sometimes no'; answers may mean different things to different respondents, so they are not comparable

Open questions

Open questions leave the answer open for the respondent to give their views. An example of an open question (sometimes called an open-ended question) is a question asking 'What do you think about...?'

Table 6 Strengths and weaknesses of open-ended questions

Strengths	Weaknesses
Respondent is not constrained but free to answer as they wish, so will give more detailed, in-depth and rich data	Difficult to analyse because tend to be interpreted by the respondent; too difficult to compare data with those of other respondents
Allows respondent to interpret the questions as they wish, so produces more valid 'real' data than when constrained by the questions	Often are not answered in full as they take longer and it is more difficult to think of the answer than when ticking a forced-choice box

Quantitative data

Quantitative data are data where numbers are collected and given scores. For example, if time is measured, that is quantitative, or if the number of 'yes' answers and the number of 'no' answers are counted, that is quantitative. Closed questions gather quantitative data. Even categories like 'strongly agree' involve scoring.

Table 7 Likert-type scale and scoring

SA: strongly agree; A: agree; DK: unsure; D: disagree; SD: strongly disagree

Statement	SA	A	DK	D	SD
I don't talk much with people outside my own group	5	4	3	2	1
I have lots of friends with the same interests	5	4	3	2	1
I like meeting people even if they are different from me	1	2	3	4	5
The table is scored 'high' for 'prefers own in-group'.					

Examiner tip

When asked to evaluate, concerning methodology issues, there are often 4 marks available. Another type of question is to ask for one strength and one weakness, with 2 marks each. Preparing two strengths and two weaknesses can help for a general evaluation question as well as for a question asking specifically for strengths and weaknesses, so it is a good study skills habit.

Examiner tip

Examination questions can ask you to make up a question. Practise thinking of an example of both an open and a closed question. For example, ask your friend an open question (such as 'How did you get on last night?') and a closed question (such as 'Did you go to Simon's house last night?'). Make sure that the open-ended question allows a free response, not a restricted one.

Knowledge check 6

How are open questions more valid and closed questions more reliable?

Examiner tip

You may have to answer the question 'What is meant by quantitative data?' (or *qualitative* data). Often there are 2 marks available, so make sure you say enough: you can add an example (which can serve as elaboration), or you can add information to a basic point.

Examiner tip

For terms such as 'open question', 'closed question', 'quantitative data' and 'qualitative data', prepare a definition or/and examples using cards or a similar system. Practise writing definitions, giving examples, making comparisons between such terms and giving a strength and a weakness.

Knowledge check 7

What is good about qualitative data compared to quantitative data?

Examiner tip

Multiple-choice questions are often asked about the three measures of central tendency. Using made-up numbers, practise working out each of the three. Mode is the fashionable number (most common), median is medium (in the middle), and mean is meanest (hardest) in terms of calculations (add them all up and divide by the number there are).

Qualitative data

Qualitative data are data about opinions and attitudes rather than numbers. They are data that tell a story in some way. Open questions gather qualitative data when they ask questions such as 'What do you think of people who do not have the same ideas as you?'

Table 8 Strengths and weaknesses of qualitative data

Strengths	Weaknesses
Allow more in-depth analysis because of greater detail	Difficult to analyse because the data can be so different that they are hard to summarise
More valid because respondents can say what they really think	There is more detail and depth and it can take longer both for the researcher and the participant

A questionnaire usually includes both open and closed questions and so gathers both quantitative (giving quantity) and qualitative (giving quality) data. A **pilot survey** is useful. This is a survey run with a few participants to test the questions and check their clarity and suitability. In the light of the pilot, changes can be made.

Collecting data using questionnaires

Questionnaires can be posted out to people, which can be quite costly and also risks producing a low response rate. However, a lot of people can be reached that way and more have the opportunity to take part. The sample would be a volunteer sample — of those who were sent the questionnaire in the first place. The questionnaires can be handed out by the researcher and completed there and then, which should improve the response rate but would limit the coverage. They can be handed out by someone else or left somewhere for completion. All these different ways of getting data mean that this is a flexible research method.

Analysis of quantitative data/closed questions

Quantitative data provide numbers, so initial analysis is by means of percentages and descriptive statistics. Descriptive statistics include **measures of central tendency**, which are the mode, median and mean averages. Graphs are also used, such as bar charts, line graphs and pie charts. The data are analysed in such a way that they can be clearly displayed and understood. Sometimes just totals are used.

Mode — the most common score in the set of scores:

    1   5   7   8   8   12   12   12   15 — the mode is 12

Median — the middle score in the set of scores:

    1   5   7   8   8   12   12   12   15 — the median is 8

    1   5   7   8   8   11   13   14   15   20 — the median is 9.5 (between 8 and 11)

Mean — the arithmetical average found by totalling all the scores in the set and dividing by the number of scores in the set:

    1   5   7   8   8   11   13   14   15   20 — the mean is 10.2 (102 divided by 10)

Analysis of qualitative data/open questions

Qualitative data are in the form of a story or comments from the respondent, so need to be summarised in some way to make them manageable and clear. This is done by generating themes from the data, such as finding that most respondents comment on liking people of the same age or on not liking people from a different social class. Themes would focus on age and class.

Analysis of questionnaires

Using the quantitative data, scores are assigned to groups obtained from the personal data. For example, scores of males and females can be separated and compared. Scores of younger and older respondents can be compared, or scores of those employed compared to those of students. This rather depends on the hypothesis/aim of the questionnaire.

The themes from the qualitative data can also be sorted into groups such as gender, age and class, depending on what the researcher wants to find out. Perhaps, for example, males talk more about class and females talk more about age.

Evaluation of questionnaires as a research method

Evaluate using the type of question and type of data

When evaluating questionnaires, you can use evaluation of the types of question (open and closed) and the types of data (qualitative and quantitative).

Open questions gather qualitative data, which are useful because they provide rich detail that can generate themes and give more in-depth analysis. Closed questions gather quantitative data, which are useful because analysis can be in the form of percentages and averages, numbers that can be compared more easily than themes.

Evaluate by looking at validity

Questionnaires can be evaluated according to their validity, which means how far what they gather is 'real-life' information.

When someone has to answer a question that has a forced choice of response (such as yes/no questions) they are restricted in their answer, so their responses are not likely to be valid. They might want to say something else entirely. This is a lack of *construct* validity (the questions don't do a good job of measuring what they are supposed to measure).

When someone is answering a questionnaire, they are doing an artificial task and so are in an artificial situation. This means the responses lack *ecological* validity (the answers are not given in a setting or situation that is natural to the respondent, so they may not be valid because of that).

Questionnaires can only find out what the respondents think is true of themselves or how they would behave. They do not measure actual behaviour. So there is a lack of validity in this sense as well.

To an extent, questionnaires are valid when they use open questions because then the respondent has some chance of saying what they 'really' think — though you

---

Examiner tip

In methodology questions, you may need to apply your understanding to 'unseen' situations. This can include analysing data presented in some format. Make up some data and practise interpretation and analysis. Note down trends such as similarities and differences and use the actual figures in your answer (percentages or fractions).

Knowledge check 8

Why would qualitative data, from open questions, in their raw form, not be suitable for using descriptive statistics?

Examiner tip

Questions asking you to evaluate can ask for strengths or weaknesses, or evaluation in general. It tends to be found that answers giving strengths do not gain as many marks as answers giving weaknesses, so when revising it is useful to focus on strengths as well as weaknesses, and in equal measure.

Examiner tip

In a question about validity, you may want to use these two different types of validity to extend your answer and add detail. Answers that reach high grades tend to have such detail and use terminology in this sort of way.

Knowledge check 9

What does it mean to say that questionnaires do not measure actual behaviour?

Examiner tip

Evaluation of one methodological issue can be used to evaluate another. For example, evaluation of closed questions — such as that they yield measurable and replicable answers so can show reliability — can be used to evaluate reliability (e.g. it is good in a questionnaire because closed questions are used). Put an evaluation term in the middle of a mind map (e.g. 'reliability') and fill in as many issues about it as you can to form a diagram you can remember.

Examiner tip

Questions asking for evaluation of a study or a research method can ask you to evaluate in terms of reliability, validity, generalisability or specifically in some way. Make sure you clearly understand such issues. For example, an extended writing/essay question might ask you to describe one of the studies you have looked at in detail (such as Hofling et al., 1966) and to evaluate it in terms of reliability and validity.

could argue that given lack of space and the demands of the question, this validity is limited.

Issues affecting validity include how truthful the answers are. **Demand characteristics** are when characteristics of a question or features of any study (demand characteristics are found in other research methods too) give clues to the respondent or participant about the answer(s) expected. Questions need to be subtle and to hide their true intention (while remembering ethical issues, which are discussed below).

Social desirability can also affect answers, as people tend to reply as they think they should reply. For example, if asked if you are a racist, you are unlikely to say yes.

Evaluate by looking at reliability

Questionnaires can be evaluated by considering how reliable they are. This means considering whether, if the questionnaire were carried out again, the same results would be found.

A pilot study would test questions for ease of understanding and usefulness with regard to achieving the questionnaire's aims, so that would help reliability. If the questions are clear, the same findings are likely to be produced if they are administered again.

Closed questions have forced-choice answers, so respondents are likely to fit themselves into the same category if asked again. This means questionnaires are a reasonably reliable method.

Questionnaires are set out and repeated exactly — they are replicable, which is a condition for reliability.

Open questions might be less reliable, as they allow for opinions to be given and opinions may differ over time and place. In one mood a respondent might answer one way, whereas in another state they might answer differently.

Evaluate by looking at generalisability

Generalisability depends on how well the sampling ensures that the people asked represent the population that is being looked at (the target population). In your course, you look at random sampling, stratified sampling, volunteer/self-selected sampling and opportunity sampling. To help you to understand these four types of sampling, as well as to understand issues of generalisability, those four are considered here with regard to questionnaires. Results are **generalisable** when they come from good sampling that represents the target population, so it can be said that what was found is 'true' of all the others who were not in the sample.

(1) **Random sampling** means that everyone in the target population or sampling frame has an equal chance of being picked to be in the sample. The target population is likely to be very large (such as everyone if you are looking at memory, perhaps), but random sampling of everyone is not possible, as not all of them would be available to be picked. The sampling frame is those who can be picked, such as all students in one sixth form, and all of those would need to be available to be chosen if the sample is random. (Two ways of doing this are names in a hat, or using random number tables and a list of all the names.) A random sample gives good generalisability because you would expect the sample to be representative of the target population and not to have bias.

(2) **Stratified sampling** means generating categories that fit the aim(s) of the study, such as age, gender, occupation, or whether someone drives or not. From these categories, people are chosen so that the sample is bound to include people from these categories. This can be generalisable because all the necessary characteristics will be in the sample, though the numbers in each category should reflect the numbers in the target population, which is not easy to do.

(3) **Volunteer/self-selected sampling** means asking people to volunteer. If a questionnaire is sent out by post, those returning it will by definition have volunteered. It is not easy to generalise from this, because there is something different about people who volunteer and select themselves for the sample. They might have strong views about the topic, for example, or have more time than other people.

(4) **Opportunity sampling** means the researcher takes whoever they can find. This can be biased because it would be anyone around at that time, which might exclude those working or those at school if the study was done on a weekday in the daytime. It is not easy to generalise from such sampling, because there is no science in how people are obtained and there is a strong element of chance and bias.

Knowledge check 10

Give one sentence each to explain random, stratified, volunteer/self-selected and opportunity sampling.

Examiner tip

Four types of sampling can be asked about directly (random, stratified, volunteer/self-selected and opportunity). Be ready to define any one of these and to discuss them with regards to their generalisability — both how they might give generalisability and how they might not, as well as preparing for other questions about them, such as their strengths and weaknesses.

Table 9 Strengths and weaknesses of simple random sampling

Strengths	Weaknesses
Low bias because everyone has an equal chance of being chosen	Cannot be certain that the sample is representative of all groups/types etc.
Sample can be checked mathematically for bias	Difficult to access all the population so that random sampling can take place

Table 10 Strengths and weaknesses of stratified sampling

Strengths	Weaknesses
All relevant groups/strata will have at least some representation	It is difficult to know how many of each group is needed in order to represent the target population accurately
Limits the numbers of participants needed	Relies on researchers knowing all the required groups/strata; forces choice of participants and proportions of all groups, so can give bias by excluding people

Table 11 Strengths and weaknesses of volunteer/self-selected sampling

Strengths	Weaknesses
Ethically good because people volunteer, so are willing to be involved	Only certain types of people may volunteer, so there is bias
More likely to cooperate, which means there may be less social desirability and such biases	May take a long time to get enough volunteers

Table 12 Strengths and weaknesses of opportunity sampling

Strengths	Weaknesses
More ethical because the researcher can judge if the participant is likely to be upset by the study or is too busy to take part	Only people available are used and they may be a self-selected group (e.g. not working, so available during the day)
The researcher has more control over who is chosen and should, therefore, be able to get the sample quickly and efficiently	May not get representatives from all groups, so there may be bias

Evaluate by looking at objectivity

Psychology is a science and as such needs to present data that are reliable and objective. Objectivity refers to avoiding bias when gathering data, particularly bias from the researcher's own opinions and understanding. Controls are used to make sure that data are objectively gathered. Controls have to cover situational and participant variables. **Experimenter/researcher effects** must also be controlled for, such as the effects of tone of voice, clothes worn or the gender or age of the researcher. This is important in a questionnaire. **Subjectivity** is to be avoided (there must be objectivity for research to be scientific, which is an aim of psychology) when data are analysed as well as when data are gathered. For example, when themes are being generated, these must come from the data, not from preconceptions of the researcher.

Evaluate by looking at credibility

Science must generate credible data. If psychology maintains that something is true which people do not believe, this is not useful. Data are credible if they are valid (true to life) and reliable (found more than once). They are credible if they can be generalised (said to be true of others, not just the sample used) and if they agree with common sense. If the evidence is carefully presented and strong, the results will be credible (usually). There are occasions when psychology puts forward a finding that is 'incredible' — such as Milgram's finding that 'ordinary' people were capable of doing 'extraordinary' things (giving what they thought were lethal electric shocks to others). If the evidence is strong enough (which Milgram's was) and relates to real life (which it did, because in the Holocaust 'ordinary' people did 'extraordinary' things), the findings are accepted in spite of their apparent lack of credibility.

Table 13 Strengths and weaknesses of questionnaires

Strengths	Weaknesses
They are often reliable because bias from the researcher can be avoided by having set questions and a set procedure	They could be administered differently by different people, so data may be biased by the situation, which would make them unreliable
If questions and procedure are set so that bias is avoided, data should be valid	If fixed questions are mainly asked, then useful relevant data can be missed, making data invalid. Respondents are not free to say what they want to say, even if open questions are chosen

Evaluate by using ethical considerations

In your course, you have studied five main ethical guidelines: informed consent, lack of deceit, right to withdraw, debriefing and competence.

Table 14 Five main ethical guidelines for your course

Guideline	Explanation
Informed consent	Participants must agree to taking part and having their data used, knowing as much as possible about the study (they consent, and it is informed consent)
Lack of deceit	There must be no deceit — participants must be fully informed. Where deceit is necessary because otherwise the study would not work, there must be a full debrief
Right to withdraw	Participants must be given the right to withdraw at any time, both during the study and afterwards, when they can withdraw their data
Debriefing	Participants must be fully informed after the study — of what it was about and where their findings fit. This is particularly important if there is deceit and, therefore, lack of informed consent
Competence	The researcher must be competent to carry out the study. They must be sufficiently qualified and/or overseen by someone else. They must adhere to ethical guidelines and understand not only what they are doing, but also the consequences, which they must be equipped to deal with

Questionnaires can have good **ethics**, because ethical considerations can be addressed on the questionnaire itself. The right to withdraw can be clearly stated, for example, as can the purpose of the study. Participants can usually be fully informed and not deceived. A debrief can also be included at the end in written form, or the researcher can explain after collecting the data. The questionnaire can be checked to make sure it is suitable and ethical, which ensures competence, although the consequences of completing the questionnaire must be considered (for example, if the topic is potentially distressing).

Later in this section, when Milgram's work is considered, you can practise using the five ethical issues in preparation for the examination.

Interviews

Surveys can be carried out using interviews as well as questionnaires. You will have looked at three types of interview: structured, semi-structured and unstructured interviews.

Table 15 Three types of interview

Type of interview	Explanation	Brief evaluation
Structured	Planned questions throughout	+ Can be repeated and data can be compared − Forced choice, so tends to lack validity
Semi-structured	Half planned, half able to explore issues	+ More valid, as can explore to get real-life answers − Can be hard to compare data if issues different

Examiner tip

Examination questions can ask specifically for evaluation of ethics (e.g. of a study), in which case only focus on ethical issues. However, be specific rather than general. For example, do not discuss Milgram's work by saying he needed to give the right to withdraw such as to suggest that though this was given, in practice participants were pressured into continuing by use of verbal prods.

Knowledge check 12

Write a few sentences that incorporate the five ethical guidelines featured in this section and show clearly what each is and why it is important.

Examiner tip

When writing about ethical issues, pay attention to how you word your answer. It is not that participants 'have' informed consent, for example, but that they must 'give' informed consent. Also, they must be given the right to withdraw and given a debrief, rather than them 'giving right to withdraw'. Make sure that the 'name' of the guideline makes sense in a sentence.

Type of interview	Explanation	Brief evaluation
Unstructured	Areas planned but questions can follow lead of respondent (looser structure)	+ More valid, as respondent leads − Less comparable and less replicable, so harder to test for reliability

A structured interview is essentially a questionnaire administered individually. An unstructured interview is much looser in format and the interviewer can explore issues. A semi-structured interview draws on both these ideas. In general, data from interviews are qualitative data, although the structured part of the interview is likely to gather quantitative data, and personal data (age, gender etc.) tend to generate quantitative data.

Interviews need a **schedule**, which is the set of questions/areas that need to be covered, whether in a fully structured or unstructured way. There also needs to be a **transcript**, which involves writing out all the replies so that data can be thoroughly and objectively analysed.

When answering questions about interviews, with regard to open and closed questions, qualitative and quantitative data, and analysis of data, use what you have learned about these issues when looking at questionnaires, as the same issues arise. There might, however, be more bias in an interview because the interviewer can feature more, so there might be researcher effects.

Knowledge check 13

Why might there be more bias in an interview than in a postal questionnaire?

Knowledge check 14

Name three types of interview and give one strength of each.

Examiner tip

What you are asked to do is set out in the assessment objectives (AOs). Part of AO3 (which relates to methodology) asks you to 'analyse, interpret, explain and evaluate'. This can include comparing. Revising material by comparing can be very useful as it can cover both knowledge and understanding (you have to know it to compare it) and evaluation (comparing involves looking at similarities and differences).

Table 16 Strengths and weaknesses of interviews

Strengths	Weaknesses
Questions can be explained and enlarged upon, so this is a good method when in-depth and detailed data are required	The interviewer may influence the data (e.g. by tone, dress, gender), which would result in researcher bias
Data tend to be valid because interviewees use their own words and are not as constrained by the questions as they are in a questionnaire	Analysis may be subjective (e.g. generating themes) and the researcher's views may influence the analysis

Table 17 Comparing questionnaires and interviews in terms of reliability, validity and subjectivity

Questionnaires	Interviews
Reliability Structured questions and the same for all respondents, so replicable and likely to be reliable	Each person interviewed separately in different settings and on different occasions and perhaps by a different person; difficult to replicate and test for reliability
Validity Set questions with forced-choice answers are likely to be less valid as may not yield 'true' data	Questions can be explained and explored, so likely to be valid and give 'real-life' and 'true' data
Subjectivity Structured format; less open to researcher bias in the analysis; closed questions do not require interpretation; open questions are likely to give short answers, so themes are clearer	Open to bias in analysis as generating themes requires interpretation; open to subjectivity, but analysis can be objective if the steps are made clear

- Surveys are a popular method in the social approach and in psychology and involve questionnaires and interviews.
- The two involve the use of open and closed questions, pilot surveys, aims and alternate hypotheses, and, for interviews, interview schedules.
- Interviews can be structured, semi-structured or unstructured and are carried out by someone rather than by post or through a written document.
- With regard to design decisions, open questions gather qualitative data and closed questions gather quantitative data.
- In general, open questions gathering qualitative data give more validity and closed questions gathering quantitative data give more reliability.
- Quantitative data, which are in the form of numbers, are analysed using descriptive statistics, which include measures of central tendency (mode, median and mean) as well as graphs and charts.
- Qualitative data, which involve detail in the form of words or pictures, for example, are analysed by generating themes and categories from the data, grouping comments and ideas to summarise and conclude.
- Both questionnaires and interviews can yield biased data, one aspect being subjectivity as the researcher's views can affect the data. Other bias that both questionnaires and interviews can suffer from include demand characteristics and social desirability, which affect the validity and reliability of the data.
- All studies in psychology, including those in social psychology, must adhere to ethical guidelines that are laid down by the British Psychological Society (and there are other bodies that have guidelines too). Five such guidelines are getting informed consent, having no deceit, giving the right to withdraw, giving a debrief at the end, and being competent to carry out the study.
- A study is generalisable only in so far as the sampling technique reflects the target population, so sampling is important. Four sampling techniques are random, stratified, volunteer/self-selected and opportunity.

Content

Within the social approach, your course covers obedience and prejudice. Here these issues are dealt with in that order.

Obedience

Obedience means to obey a direct order from an authority figure: an example is a soldier obeying orders. Conformity is different: it means you *agree* with carrying out the action. Obedience and compliance both mean following orders when you do not necessarily agree.

A main name in the study of obedience is Milgram. He carried out a number of studies, the main one of which was in 1963, where he ordered participants to 'shock' someone. You need to know his basic study and at least one of the variations of that study.

Milgram's 1963 basic study

Aim

Milgram aimed to test the idea that 'Germans were different' when they carried out orders to persecute Jews and others during the Second World War. How far would 'ordinary people' go if ordered to administer what they thought were electric shocks to someone else? (He found that Germans are not different — others obeyed 'shocking' orders too.)

Examiner tip
You will find in the glossary terms such as 'obedience'. These terms are not always defined in great detail in the Content Guidance section, so use the glossary as a revision guide and add detail from there to inform preparation for 'definition' questions. You could use index cards to put a term on one side and a definition with an example on the other and aim for a 3-mark question.

Procedure

Through an advertisement, 40 men were obtained who were willing to take part. The laboratory experiment took place at Yale, a well-regarded university. There was a room with a generator and levers. The levers had labels showing a range of voltages from 15 volts upwards and indicating from mild to severe shock and 'danger'. In another room was a chair that appeared to be wired up. The implication was clear: the generator delivered shocks and the person in the chair received the voltage on the label. There was an accomplice, whom the participants thought was another volunteer. The accomplice was placed in the chair and 'wired up'. He was primed to shout out at certain points and then to go (ominously) quiet. In the meantime, the participant, who thought that he had been chosen as a 'teacher' and that the accomplice was just the 'learner' by chance (although in fact the draw was rigged), was seated at the generator and told what to do. The participant had to read out word pairs, which the accomplice had to 'learn' and be tested on. The accomplice, of course, was told to answer incorrectly sometimes, so that the teacher had to give 'shocks'. The teacher was told to increase the 'shock' by 15 volts at each wrong answer. The accomplice could be heard and not seen. The participant started the experiment and duly administered the shocks. Each participant was tested separately. If the participant protested and stopped, the experimenter said things like 'You must go on'. These instructions were called 'verbal prods'. After the fourth prod, if the participant still refused to go on, the experiment was stopped. After a time, the accomplice was silent — he could have been injured or even be dead.

Table 18 Some main issues in the procedure

Issue	Comment
The participants were volunteers	This made the sample biased — look at strengths and weaknesses of volunteer samples as outlined earlier
The participants were deceived	They were told it was a study of memory but it was about obedience. They were told that the accomplice was another participant, but he was not. They were told that the 'shocks' were real and they were not
The participants were not given the right to withdraw fully	They could stop but there were four prods first, which is not in accordance with current guidelines
The experimenter was in the room	They may have felt obliged to continue just because the experimenter was present — and supposedly making sure no harm was done to the 'accomplice'
The study was at Yale University	This is a well-known university with a lot of prestige. The participants would expect things to be under control

Results

Participants protested — but there was a script, and each time they protested the experimenter followed this script. All of them (100%) went up to 300 volts. Then some stopped and would not go on. However, 26 of the 40 men (65%) carried on to the end, which was 450 volts. During the study, many participants were very distressed and one even had what was called a full-blown seizure.

Conclusions

Milgram concluded that an ordinary person would obey orders from an authority to an extreme extent even when they were very uncomfortable about doing so.

Table 19 Strengths and weaknesses of the basic study by Milgram (1963)

Strengths	Weaknesses
Good controls avoid bias and mean that the situation was the same for all, so cause-and-effect conclusions could be drawn	The study is unethical because the participants were deceived, did not give informed consent, were distressed and did not have the full right to withdraw
The well-controlled procedures mean that the study is replicable and can be tested for reliability	The study lacks validity because of the artificial procedures

Variations of Milgram's 1963 study

You need to know one of the variations of the main study.

Aims of variations

Milgram wanted to investigate reasons for the high level of obedience in a systematic way, so he changed one variable at a time to see what the effect was. Each variation had a separate aim which was to see:

- the effect of the study being at Yale, a prestigious university
- the effect of the victim being remote from the participant
- the effect of the experimenter being in the room
- what would happen if others were there, and they refused at some stage
- what would happen if there were two experimenters, one of whom told the participant to stop

Procedures and results of variations

- Moving the study to a run-down office block gave 47.5% obedience to 450 volts.
- Having the participant hold down the victim's hand to receive the shock gave 30% obedience to 450 volts.
- Not having the experimenter in the room and orders given over the phone, gave 22.5% obedience to 450 volts.
- Having two colleagues who both refused before 300 volts meant only 10% obedience to 450 volts.
- When one experimenter told the participant to stop and the other said continue, none of the participants continued to 450 volts.

Agency theory

Milgram suggested that participants in his studies were in an agentic state, which means that they acted as agents of the experimenter even though they were under moral strain. Moral strain refers to the pressure of doing something against one's feelings of right and wrong, and an agentic state is when a person is acting because someone else is in authority, rather than acting as an individual. When acting as an

> **Examiner tip**
>
> When learning studies and preparing to answer questions about them, it is a good idea to prepare enough for 2 marks for the aim, 6 marks for the procedure, 4 marks for the results and 4 marks for conclusions for each study you are covering. Then prepare enough for 4 marks on strengths and 4 marks on weaknesses so that you can evaluate a study when asked. Remember a 'mark' means giving a point clearly and in some detail.

> **Knowledge check 15**
>
> Give three reasons for Milgram's 1963 study being well thought of in terms of methodology.

> **Examiner tip**
>
> It can be customary in textbooks to briefly outline Milgram's variations and give the effect on the results, which is how the variations are presented here. However, you need to know one of the variations in some detail, so make sure you can describe one of Milgram's variations as well as evaluate it.

individual, a person is in an autonomous state. There is an evolutionary aspect to agency theory. It is likely that humans who worked in a hierarchical social system were more apt to survive. For example, an individual on their own might be more susceptible to predators, so less likely to survive. It is also probable that there is a learned aspect to being in an agentic state, as schools and other social systems rely on power structures and on people obeying those in authority.

Table 20 Strengths and weaknesses of agency theory as an explanation for obedience

Strengths of agency theory	Weaknesses of agency theory
The findings of the variations on Milgram's study back up the theory, because the less they were agents (for example, when the experimenter was not in the room), the less they obeyed	Social power theory is an alternative explanation. In Milgram's studies, the experimenter had reward power, legitimate power and expert power, so could have been obeyed because of being powerful
The theory helps to explain real-life situations such as the Holocaust, where obedience was well beyond what would be expected of autonomous human beings	The theory is more a description than an explanation. Obedience is defined as obeying an authority figure, so saying that people obey because they are agents of an authority figure does not add much

Study of obedience in a country other than the USA

Here you have a choice of study, but Meeus and Raaijmakers (1986) is suggested for your course and is the chosen study here. This is a study that took place in the Netherlands and is sometimes referred to here as 'the Dutch study'.

Aim

The aim of Meeus and Raaijmakers was to make the situation more real by using psychological violence. They wanted their participants to believe that they were doing definite harm to the victim. Their study used the kind of violence that might be found in Western societies. They also carried out a second study with the aim of seeing if two variations would reduce obedience, as Milgram's variations did. The two variations were:

- a study with the experimenter absent
- a study with two peer-confederates present, i.e. three people administering the punishment

General procedure

Meeus and Raaijmakers used a university researcher, the participant and someone applying for a job, so there were three people, as in Milgram's study. The applicant was a trained accomplice who had come to the laboratory to take a test; if he 'passed' the test, he got the job. The participant had to interrupt the applicant by making 'stress remarks', that is, negative remarks about the applicant's performance and personality. Participants were told that being able to work under pressure was a requirement of the job for which the applicant was applying. They were also told that the procedure was to help the experimenter's research into the relationship between psychological stress and test achievement. The applicant objected to the interruptions. The participants were told to ignore these objections, which increased as the procedure continued. Due to the stress remarks, the applicant 'failed' the test and 'did not get the job'. The dilemma here for the participant is whether scientific research should affect someone's job and career. The question is whether the participants will cooperate. There were two studies: one is the main study, the other uses the two variations.

Table 21 Procedure for Experiment 1

39 participants, aged 18–55 years, both males and females, at least Dutch high school education.
Volunteer sample through newspaper advertisements, paid a small amount, 24 in an experimental group and 15 in a control group.
Experiment was in a modern building, university campus, male experimenter about 30 years old, well dressed and friendly though stern.
The 'applicant', in a different room listening via a speaker, took a test consisting of 32 multiple-choice questions read out to him.
The participant thought that the applicant was doing a real test for a real job.
The participant had to give 15 negative remarks during the test; a TV screen told him/her when to make the remarks and what to say.
Electrodes on the applicant's skull measured tension, which was displayed numerically for the participant to see, and he/she was also told verbally about the applicant's stress levels (e.g. 'normal' or 'intense').
The participant heard the applicant ask whether cooperating with the study would affect test performance; the applicant was told it would not, so the participant believed the applicant was lied to.
If the participant refused to continue, there were four verbal prods, just as in Milgram's study.

Table 22 Procedure for Experiment 2

41 participants, 22 in the 'experimenter absent' condition and 19 in the 'two peers rebel' condition.
The 'experimenter absent' condition was when the experimenter set up the study, ordered the stress remarks and then left the room.
The 'two peers rebel' condition was when the real participant was with two other 'participants', who in fact were confederates. After stress remark 8 (out of 15), both confederates started protesting. After stress remark 10, both confederates stopped making the remarks and the participant was asked to continue.

Results of Experiment 1

91.7% of the participants were obedient and made all the stress remarks (i.e. 22 of the 24 participants obeyed to the end). None of those in the control group made *all* the stress remarks. Participants discussed whether to continue or not with the experimenter but obeyed without much protest. Follow-up procedures showed that participants were upset by the study. 73% of the participants believed that the study was authentic (they believed that the applicant was really applying for the job and that what they were doing was as it was suggested to them), 23% were not sure about its authenticity and 4% thought it was a hoax. As for the responsibility of harm done to the applicant, the participants thought that 45% of it was down to the experimenter, 33% to the participant and 22% to the applicant.

Knowledge check 17

In a single sentence, describe the results of Meeus and Raaijmakers' study (Experiment 1), accurately incorporating the three percentages given.

Results of Experiment 2

Obedience was lower in both the situations ('experimenter absent' and 'two peers rebel') compared with Experiment 1. 36.4% were fully obedient (made all the stress remarks) in the 'experimenter absent' condition, while 15.8% were fully obedient in the 'two peers rebel' condition. In each of the conditions, just over 80% believed the experimental set up.

Conclusions

Clearly the Dutch study found obedience, as did Milgram, and in fact obedience was much higher than in Milgram's study. And as with Milgram, the two variations showed lower levels of obedience. So the study supports Milgram's conclusions: even in a different culture and at a different time, high obedience was found, even though participants found obeying distressing. In Experiment 1, approximately half the participants blamed the experimenter for the harm done to the applicant, as if they were agents of the experimenter rather than acting autonomously, which is support for agency theory.

Table 23 Strengths and weaknesses of the study by Meeus and Raaijmakers (1986)

Strengths	Weaknesses
Deliberately planned so that comparisons could be made with Milgram's studies, which means the results are more interesting and useful	There are differences between the Milgram and Dutch studies, not only the planned differences (e.g. the studies are in different cultures and nearly 15 years apart)
The controls and careful planning mean that the study is replicable and can be tested for reliability, and cause-and-effect conclusions are more easily made	The situation is not valid, in that the applicant is in a laboratory taking a test for a job, which is not a natural situation

Drawing cross-cultural conclusions about obedience

Compare Milgram's main study and one of his variations with Meeus and Raaijmakers' study, including considering whether differences in culture affected differences in findings.

Table 24 Comparing Milgram's work with Meeus and Raaijmakers'

Issue	Comparison point
Type of punishment	Milgram asked for physical punishment to be administered (but pretend) and the Dutch study asked for psychological punishment (in more ways real, but still set up).
Obedience level for main study	The Dutch study found a much higher level of full obedience. Milgram found 65% whereas Meeus and Raaijmakers found 91.7%.
Obedience level with two peers present	Milgram found that 10% obeyed in this condition, compared with 15.8% in the Dutch study.

Issue	Comparison point
Obedience when experimenter was absent	Milgram found 22.5% obedience and the Dutch study found 36.4%.
General comparison of obedience levels	The Dutch study found a higher level of obedience in all three conditions. This could be because of the different type of punishment, the different country or the different time (1986 instead of 1963).
Effect of different type of punishment	The 'shocks' were less remote than the psychological punishment. For example, Milgram's participants heard screams and felt a slight shock too.
Other differences between the two studies	In the Dutch study, the participants had agreed to harm the applicants, but Milgram's participants had not agreed. So in the Dutch study the participants might have felt they should continue because they had agreed to. Consent levels were different.
Agency theory	Both studies support the idea of agency theory because in both cases, although the participants were clearly distressed when taking part, they continued. It seems that this was not autonomous decision making. Participants were less obedient without the experimenter there, which suggests that at least in part they were acting as an agent of the experimenter.

It is hard to show that the greater obedience in the Dutch study was because of it being in a different country, because there were other differences too. It is possible that either a different culture or a different time in history affected the findings, but to find this out a study would have to be perfectly replicated, and Meeus and Raaijmakers made important changes to Milgram's study. They conclude that there is still high obedience to authority more than 20 years after Milgram and in a different situation. This suggests that it is not culture that gives obedience or norms of a society, but that obedience is something that would be found in any culture at any time. Perhaps this supports the evolutionary element of agency theory. Note, though, that the Netherlands and the USA are not completely different cultures.

Ethical issues arising from obedience studies

You need to know about ethical issues in psychology, including those arising from obedience studies. There are five main ethical issues in your course.

Consent

- Milgram's participants gave consent to a study about learning, but not to a study about obedience and not to give what they thought were strong electric shocks to someone else. So the consent was not informed.
- Meeus and Raaijmakers informed participants what they were going to be doing and obtained consent, so in that way the Dutch study was more ethical. However, there was some deception, as explained below, so there was some limit to the informed nature of the consent.

Examiner tip
Short answers to an examination question are not always the best and can be incorrect. For example, you might argue that the differences in obedience levels found between Meeus and Raaijmakers and Milgram are because the studies were done in different cultures. However, you would need to elaborate on the differences between the cultures (you could equally argue that they are the same) and also explain that there were other differences (you could equally well argue that there were similarities).

Deceit

- Milgram deceived his participants in a number of ways. They thought the study was about learning, whereas it was about obedience. They thought that the person receiving the 'shocks' was a participant too, though he was really an accomplice. More importantly, they thought that the 'shocks' were real.
- Meeus and Raaijmakers gave more information to their participants, but there was deceit because the participants thought the job applicant was really applying for a job that would affect his future, whereas the job applicant was a confederate. The responses to the stress remarks were set up too, which was also deceit.

Right to withdraw

- Milgram took away some of his participants' right to withdraw because he used four different verbal prods to keep the participant obeying. When the participant objected, he did not immediately let them withdraw from the study. To an extent participants did have the right to withdraw, and indeed some participants did withdraw from the study: after the fourth verbal prod, if the participant still objected, the study was ended.
- Meeus and Raaijmakers also used verbal prods — four as well, to replicate Milgram's study — so they too took away the right to withdraw immediately. Again, to an extent there was a right to withdraw: after the fourth verbal prod, as in Milgram's study.

Competence

- Milgram was competent to carry out the study. He also asked the opinion of colleagues about the study, which increased the level of competence.
- Meeus and Raaijmakers were also competent in terms of where they worked and their experience. They also used Milgram's experiences to learn from.

Knowledge check 18

Explain two ethical similarities or differences (use two of the five guidelines here) between Milgram's work on obedience and Meeus and Raaijmakers's study.

Debrief

- Milgram fully debriefed the participants and introduced them to their 'victim', to show that all was well. He set up interviews so that there was support for the participants. Many of them said they were happy to have taken part.
- Meeus and Raaijmakers also fully debriefed their participants, informing them about the whole study. The researchers do not say any more about ethics, but it has to be assumed that this debrief was thorough and that support was offered.

Other ethical issues with the studies

- The participants were paid in both studies, which is unethical as it means there is a contract, which the participants may not feel able to break even though they clearly want to. However, at least they were rewarded.
- There was initially confidentiality and the names of the participants were not published.
- The participants were volunteers recruited through newspaper advertisements (for both Milgram's study and the Dutch study), and this seems more ethical as they chose to take part.

- If a participant became distressed, as one did in Milgram's study, observers stepped in to stop the study, which helped to make the study ethical.
- Milgram consulted other people and it was not thought that they would find such a high level of obedience, so he did not intend the study to be as stressful for the participants as it was. Meeus and Raaijmakers, however, knew that the participants would obey (or at least would have had strong reasons to think that there would be high obedience), so perhaps their study was more unethical.
- Ethical guidelines were not as strong in 1963 as they were in 1986, or as they are today, so it is hard to judge the studies by current ethical guidelines. However, it is still useful to do so when considering whether the study was ethical or not.

Ethical issues because of useful applications

- It could be argued that a study should be carried out if the findings can be useful in making society 'better' for people. Milgram's study found that people obey an authority figure to a high level of obedience and that people act as agents of others. The Dutch study found an even higher level of obedience. Knowing this, when people in authority give orders, they now know that others will act as their agents and that they have responsibility for the orders they give. The key issue picks up this idea.

Prejudice

Another area studied within social psychology is prejudice. You need to know what prejudice is, what discrimination is and about the social identity theory of prejudice.

Definitions

- Prejudice is an attitude that is usually negative and means prejudging someone without knowing them. Prejudice is when a judgement is made about someone based on some characteristic (such as race, gender or occupation). Usually it is taken to mean making a negative judgement.
- Discrimination is when action is taken due to prejudice.

Tajfel's social identity theory as an explanation of prejudice

Social identity theory (SIT) is just one theory of prejudice. The theory suggests that prejudice arises simply from there being two groups. The idea is that our in-group, which is the group we belong to, gives us our self-esteem and identity. To enhance our self-esteem we tend to see those in other groups (the out-groups) negatively — we are prejudiced against them. According to the theory, each of us has several 'selves' according to the different groups we belong to. Our social identity comes from belonging to groups, which means we categorise ourselves as being a member of an in-group. This leads to in-group favouritism and hostility towards the out-group.

Social categorisation is seeing oneself as part of a group. Social identification is identifying with the group. Social comparison is comparing oneself with members of the out-group. As a person's self-concept is wrapped up in the group, they will enhance their self-esteem by seeing their group as better than the out-group.

Examiner tip

Fully explain each ethical point you make. For example, saying that both studies involved deceit is not enough: you need to show *how* deceit was present in each case. It is also useful to prepare more material than you think might be asked. If you expect a 4-mark answer on the ethics of Milgram's study, prepare enough for 6 to 8 marks (you are not likely to remember everything you revise, so prepare more than you need).

Knowledge check 19

What is the difference between prejudice and discrimination?

Examiner tip

For the social approach, you need to be able to define certain terms, including in-group, out-group, social categorisation, social identification and social comparison. Make sure that you know what these terms mean and that you can provide an example for each. There might be 3 marks (per definition) that you can get by preparing earlier rather than depending on thinking up an answer during the exam.

Examiner tip

Use past papers to see the number of marks that are likely to be given to theories, studies, evaluation questions and so on. Then add around another 2 marks and prepare accordingly. This helps to know how much detail is needed. For studies, 6 description marks and 6 evaluation marks would be a good starting point. Note, though, that parts of a study can be focused on, such as 4 marks for a procedure, so pay careful attention to such details.

Table 25 Strengths and weaknesses of social identity theory as an explanation of prejudice

Strengths of social identity theory	Weaknesses of social identity theory
There is a lot of evidence to show that people denigrate an out-group and show in-group favouritism. For example, Lalonde (1992) showed how even when members of a team know they are not playing very well they will still unfairly blame another team for their lack of success.	Another theory, realistic conflict theory, suggests that not only must there be two groups but they must be in conflict over resources. Lalonde (1992) studied a hockey team that was competing in a tournament, for example, not 'just' two unconnected groups.
The theory is useful and can be applied to real-life situations such as football violence and racial tension.	There are other factors involved in prejudice, not just two groups. For example, in some cases groups co-exist without problems and in others they do not. Prejudice is complex and studies find it hard to capture this complexity, so perhaps findings are not valid.

Summary

- Obedience is doing what an authority figure says and can be explained using agency theory: we act as agents of those in authority over us, even if that causes us moral strain. When not in an agentic state, we are in an autonomous state and make our own decisions.

- Milgram did a main experiment and found that participants would give what they thought were dangerous levels of shock to someone they thought was another participant. This was a very unexpected finding. When Milgram had asked his colleagues beforehand, they had not predicted the level of obedience that he found.

- Milgram did variations and found less obedience in different scenarios but still found people were willing to give the 'shocks'. It seemed that the less the participant felt they were agents of the authority

- figure or the less they 'saw' the authority, the lower their level of obedience was.

- Obedience studies have been done in countries other than the USA. Meeus and Raaijmakers found a high level of obedience in the Netherlands in the 1980s, where participants would administer psychological punishment.

- Obedience studies raise ethical issues.

- Just as obedience studies and theories (e.g. agency) can be useful to explain why 'ordinary' people can do 'extraordinary' things on being told to by someone in authority, so studies and theories about prejudice can be used to explain hostility between groups.

- Social identity theory explains that just having an in-group and an out-group can bring about prejudice through various processes.

Knowledge check 20

How would you explain prejudice between two sports teams using social identity theory?

Two studies in detail

You need to know in detail Hofling et al.'s (1966) study of nurses and their obedience to a 'doctor'. You also need to know one other study from three specified on your course. The study chosen here is Reicher and Haslam (2003, 2006). Consider, however, revising the study chosen in your course (which could be Tajfel et al. or Sherif).

Hofling et al. (1966) study of doctor–nurse relationships

Aim

Hofling et al. (1966) aimed to study obedience in a real-life situation because they wanted to know more about hospital procedures and they thought there was an issue where a nurse would go against her professional training if asked to by a doctor (someone in higher authority). They wondered how far nurses would obey doctors. Their specific aim was to see if nurses would obey an order they thought came from a doctor, even though by obeying, the nurses would be going against their training.

Procedure

The study used someone pretending to be a doctor (who was not known to the nurses), who phoned to ask for a dose of a drug to be given to a patient. The procedure was chosen so that the nurses would have to go against their professional training. The nurses should have checked up on the doctor, who was not known to them. The amount was clearly an overdose, as labelled on the bottle. They did not know the drug — it was not on the approved list. Finally, they should not have taken orders over the phone. The study used 22 wards and one nurse from each, thus 22 participants, all female (nurses tended to be female at that time).

Alongside the experiment part of the study, two other groups of nurses completed a questionnaire asking what they would do in the circumstances (the situation was exactly the same as in the field experiment). One group of nurses surveyed consisted of 12 graduate nurses and another group was of 21 student nurses. For the questionnaires, analysis involved checking how many nurses said they would obey, and for the field experiment data were gathered by checking how many nurses actually obeyed. For the field experiment, an observer watched the nurse and the study was stopped when they complied with the order or when they refused — or indeed if the participant was upset or could not find the medication. The observer also interviewed the nurse when they stopped the study, so that there could be debriefing and discussion.

Results

From the field experiment, it was found that 21 of the 22 nurses went to give the medication as ordered. Eleven of the nurses said they did not notice that the amount ordered was an overdose, but they still broke other rules, as outlined above in the procedure. None of the nurses asked for written confirmation, although several asked the doctor to appear promptly. Eighteen of the nurses indicated that they knew they were wrong to obey a telephone order but said this happened often. Sixteen nurses felt they should not have obeyed and some felt guilty or angry. From the questionnaire completed by student nurses, it was found that 21 out of 21 said they would not have given the medication and 19 of them noticed the excessive dosage. The questionnaire completed by graduate nurses showed that 10 of the 12 said they would not have given the medication.

Conclusions

It was clear that in the field experiment there was almost complete obedience, whereas in the surveys there was almost complete lack of obedience. What the nurses said on the questionnaire they would do differed from what they did in reality. Even when they obeyed, it was clear that the nurses knew they were breaking rules, but they said it was done often. The doctor–nurse relationship was strong enough to overcome the nurses' professional training. Hofling et al. concluded that, where there were two intelligences (the trained nurse and the trained doctor), in reality there was only one intelligence, which meant less good patient care. Nurses should be encouraged to use their own training and knowledge. It is a valuable trait that nurses obey doctors, but there is also a potential problem with regard to patient care. The nurses were upset by the study, which prompts questions about the ethics of it, although the aim was to help patients and to improve care, which is an ethically sound aim.

Table 26 Strengths and weaknesses of the study by Hofling et al. (1966)

Strengths	Weaknesses
The study was carried out in the nurses' natural setting, so there was ecological validity	There are ethical issues in the study because the nurses were upset that they had been observed and tested without their permission
There were clear controls so the study could be replicated to test for reliability; the results could be said to be because of the situation as set up, rather than other factors	The study was carried out in 1966, so the findings may not apply in the twenty-first century because doctor–nurse relationships are different

Reicher and Haslam (2003, 2006) study of formation of in-groups, focusing on prisoners and guards

Aims

Reicher and Haslam studied the idea of social identification and they wanted to test it experimentally. Their aim was to find a more ethical and valid way to study such behaviour other than using a laboratory experiment. Their main aim was to investigate tyranny, which they defined as being an unequal system where one group has power (usually oppressive) over another group. A more specific aim was to see if permeability between the two groups (prisoners and guards) would mean no in-group/out-group behaviour, but when the groups were impermeable, then in-groups would form. What they meant by permeability was that people could move between the groups, so when a group is impermeable it is fixed and the people remain in that group.

Procedure

The researchers worked with the BBC to set up a case study where there was a mock-up prison, prisoners and guards, and observers to see what would happen. The BBC would film the whole experiment (the researchers call it an experimental

Knowledge check 21

List three results found and three conclusions drawn by Hofling et al. (1966).

Examiner tip

Take care in the way you express yourself in an exam answer. You might be tempted to say that Hofling et al. (1966) has good reliability because the study has controls. However, reliability is only found when a study is redone and replicated. All we should really say is that because the study has clear controls, it is *replicable* and so can be *tested for* reliability. Practise giving this sort of accuracy in your answers.

Knowledge check 22

What are three aims of Reicher and Haslam in this study?

case study) and some programmes would be broadcast showing the study and what happened. The programmes were broadcast in 2002 and the study has been written up a few times since then. They called their research an experimental case study, as they manipulated variables such as whether a group was impermeable or permeable.

Some 332 participants answered an advertisement and volunteered to take part, and after thorough screening processes and assessment, 27 men were chosen. They were all men because it was easier to provide facilities for one gender and they were all chosen because they were well-adjusted and prosocial, as a baseline measure. For example, if the study found aggression, it could be shown that this aggression came from the study. From the 27, 15 were chosen in order to have a spread of age, class and race. The 15 were matched into five groups of three, and from each of these five groups a guard was chosen randomly, leaving 10 prisoners.

Many sources of data were gathered. Video recordings and tape recordings came from the BBC work. The researchers also measured cortisol levels to check for stress, and they carried out tests to look at issues such as depression, compliance and authoritarianism (how right-wing the prisoners were, for example). The guards were told what to do to an extent — they had to carry out a roll call, allocate work duties and ensure that the prison ran smoothly. The prisoners were not given any instructions.

Permeability was set up by promoting a prisoner after three days and making sure the prisoners knew from the first day that this would happen. Impermeability was set up by having no other promotions and letting the participants know this. The researchers also studied cognitive alternatives — different ways of thinking about a situation — and to do this they introduced one of the prisoners later (so only nine were there at the start). This late entry would bring in new ideas.

Ethics of the study

The researchers took great care over the ethics of the study. They set up a group of five people as an ethics committee to oversee the study and they also discussed the procedure with colleagues, so there was competence. Participants went through a thorough screening and were told all about the study, so there was informed consent to a large extent. The participants were told they could become stressed and there were two clinical psychologists on hand to monitor individuals. They could ask for a participant to be withdrawn at any time.

Results

In general, the guards failed to identify together as a group, and so did the prisoners for the first 3 days. But after the groups became impermeable (fixed), the prisoners did set up rules and norms and formed an in-group. The prisoners saw that the guards had not formed a group and eventually became stronger than the guards, thus overthrowing the structure. By day 6 the prisoners broke out of their cells and took over the guards' quarters. Then the whole group decided to run the prison as a commune, but after a few days this did not work, so the group chose strict rules instead. This was against the rules of the study, so it was stopped at that stage.

> **Knowledge check 23**
>
> Give two features of the study that make it an experiment and two features that make it a case study.

> **Examiner tip**
>
> When asked to describe a study that represents a particular research method, think carefully about which study to include. Reicher and Haslam could be called a field study — the mock prison was supposed to represent a real-life prison — or it could be called a lab study — the situation was not natural (not a real prison) and not in the participants' natural setting (they were not real prisoners). Make sure your chosen study fits the question.

> **Examiner tip**
>
> When answering a question about results of a study, give some relevant detail. For example, when there are numbers involved (quantitative data), provide the meaningful ones. Prisoners did not identify themselves as a group for the first 3 days, for example. The study itself offers more detail than is given here, so you might like to look it up in preparation.

Examiner tip

When writing conclusions, make sure they are different from the results and vice versa. The results will be the detail and the conclusion the summary. A result is that the prisoners formed themselves into a group once there was no swapping possible between the groups, but had not formed a group in the first 3 days. A conclusion is that the study supports social identity theory in that an in-group developed.

Knowledge check 24

In Reicher and Haslam's study, what steps were taken to ensure ethical procedures were used?

Conclusions

The researchers found that groups are formed because of shared norms and values. But when the groups fail, people agree to accept a strong social order even if this goes against their own values. So it is not that tyranny develops because of group behaviour and groups forming, but that tyranny develops when groups fail (the opposite). The study supports social identity theory because it showed that in-groups develop with their own norms and values, and group members categorise themselves in groups and identify with the group. However, the guards did not form a group — it was thought that this was because they did not want to be seen as authoritarian, since that is against social norms and they would be seen on television. This suggests that making behaviour visible may prevent tyranny. It was also found that the guards, who did not form a strong group, showed more mental health problems because of the study, which suggests that mental state is affected by how well groups work.

Table 27 Strengths and weaknesses of Reicher and Haslam (2006)

Strengths	Weaknesses
The study used multiple methods of collecting the data, so the data could be compared for reliability (if the same results were found by different means) and validity (if the same results were found it is more likely that behaviour was 'real life')	It was difficult to claim that the interventions caused the behaviour — for example, the prisoners may not have gained a group identity because of the impermeability of the groups but because of other factors, such as not knowing what would happen next; the researchers acknowledge this weakness
The study was set up to adhere to ethical guidelines — for example, with regard to competence, two ethical committees were consulted and one was especially set up for the duration of the study	The study was televised, which probably affected the behaviour; this could be seen as a strength, because in society people are observed; however, it could be what led to the behaviour, rather than the situation itself

Summary

- Hofling et al. (1966) carried out a field experiment to see whether nurses would obey a doctor's orders even when such orders went against their training.
- Hofling et al.'s findings about obedience to those in authority (nurses obeyed doctors) reinforce Milgram's findings about obedience to authority and fit the agency theory explanation of such obedience.
- Hofling et al.'s findings cannot necessarily be used today because the study was done in 1966, when hospitals were very different from what they are today. One difference is that nurses tended to be female (all the participants were female) and doctors male, so gender differences now might yield different conclusions.
- Another weakness of Hofling et al.'s study is an ethical one. The nurses were put into a position where they either had to obey and go against the rules or disobey and go against the rules.
- Reicher and Haslam studied in-group/out-group behaviour rather than obedience. They were looking at tyranny, which is to do with abuse of power over someone.
- Reicher and Haslam set up a mock prison and grouped one set of participants into prisoners and the other into guards who had power over the prisoners.
- They found that (possibly because the group could change) at first the two groups did not form in-groups with special norms of behaviour, but later (when the groups became impermeable) the prisoners did form into an in-group.
- The guards did not form an in-group. This could have been because it was the more unenviable group to be in — socially they did not feel good about giving orders to others.

One key issue

You need to know one key issue that can be explained using concepts and ideas from the approach, and you also need to be ready to explain an issue that you are given in the examination. Therefore, you need to be able to use what you have learned for the social approach to explain real-life issues. One issue is explained here, and more issues are given as examples in the exam questions section to help you.

Blind obedience to authority in a prison setting — Abu Ghraib

The Abu Ghraib prison is in Iraq and was used by the Iraqi government as a prison for many years. When the Iraqi government was removed from power, the prison was used for Iraqi detainees who were guarded by soldiers from the USA. In April 2004, newspapers were filled with photographs and descriptions of the torture of the Iraqi detainees and there was public condemnation of what was clearly unacceptable treatment of them. When people obey orders against their own moral code, this is seen as blind obedience, and it was assumed that the actions of the US soldiers, which dehumanised the Iraqis, were against their own moral code. The issue here is: why would the soldiers carry out these acts? Was it blind obedience to authority? Should the soldiers be charged with unlawful acts? Were the soldiers being brutal rather than 'just' obeying orders?

Social psychology can help to explain the brutality in the Abu Ghraib prison in 2004. Milgram's study showed that 65% of the participants gave 'electric shocks' to someone else because they were told to by someone in authority, which suggests that the soldiers would obey orders to torture their Iraqi prisoners because they would be obeying an authority figure. Milgram's participants were very distressed by what they were doing but they still continued. This suggests that the US soldiers would continue to obey orders even though this went against their own moral code and caused moral strain.

Haney et al. carried out a study where participants were allocated to be prisoners or guards and then ran a mock prison. They found that the guards were brutal towards the prisoners — so much so that the study had to be stopped early. This also suggests that the US soldiers would act as guards if put in that role, and it was thought that the situation itself in the Haney et al. study led to the brutality. Zimbardo, who ran the prison in the Haney et al. study, appeared in court as a witness to explain the Abu Ghraib obedience, because he believes that a situation can lead to brutality — that it was not the fault of the soldiers.

Reicher and Haslam found that when groups do not form successfully a situation can lead to tyranny, and this may have occurred in the Abu Ghraib prison. Social identity theory would suggest that when there is a strong in-group, as would be expected among the US soldiers, there is likely to be in-group favouritism and out-group hostility, and this theory could also explain the brutality in the prison.

Hofling et al. (1966) studied how nurses obeyed doctors even when such obedience was against their professional training, which adds to the idea that the US soldiers would

Examiner tip

Make sure you understand the issue as well as the explanation. Form the issue into a question so that you are clearly presenting something that needs explaining, which is what an issue is. The issue here is the prison, the detainees, the brutality and society wanting an explanation for such acts, which must surely go against the soldier's moral code in each case. Why did the soldiers blindly obey?

Knowledge check 25

Choose a key issue to prepare for the exam and give at least 4 points of description of this issue.

obey orders even if it meant committing very brutal acts. The idea of blind obedience can be explained using agency theory, because soldiers are trained to be agents of authority and agents of society and, as soldiers, they would be agents obeying orders rather than autonomous individuals. These arguments from social psychology all suggest that the US soldiers as individuals were not responsible for their actions, but in law, when such behaviour occurs it is usual for the individual to be blamed.

Summary

- A key issue that relates to social psychology is something that society wants explaining or dealing with and an issue involves a question more than a statement, for example 'what is the explanation for...'
- One key issue is that of obedience to authority figures to an extent that goes against a society's moral rules. One example was where US soldiers acted brutally towards Iraqi prisoners in their 'care'. This example can be used because trials have been held and the reported acts shown to be true.
- This issue is about what happened in Abu Ghraib. Apparently ordinary people (soldiers) did extraordinary things. This is what Milgram found to be the case in his well-known 1963 study, where he found participants would 'give electric shocks' (they were not real but the participants did not know this) to a 'victim'.
- Milgram used agency theory to suggest that the obedience was to an authority figure and the

individual went against their own moral code because they became an agent of the authority figure. In Abu Ghraib, the soldiers could have obeyed orders because they were agents of those 'above' them in authority.
- Reicher and Haslam's study backed up Tajfel's findings about in-group/out-group behaviour. These findings suggest that the soldiers as a strong in-group would show hostility to the Iraqi prisoners (the out-group) and this would raise the soldiers' self-esteem.
- Hofling et al. (1966) found that nurses obeyed doctors even when it went against their training, such as not taking orders over the phone or not using drugs that were not registered (though they were trained to obey doctors). Soldiers are trained to obey officers, so the obedience that Hofling et al. found could be the same obedience as was found in Abu Ghraib and could be how society is set up (with some in authority and some acting as agents).

Examiner tip

List concepts from what is given here (e.g. agency theory and social identity theory) and use them to explain another key issue, such as football violence. You will find that the concepts and ideas you have studied — such as agency theory, in-group and out-group behaviour and findings of obedience studies — will be useful in explaining many issues, so learn them ready for the exam in case you are presented with a new issue to explain.

Practical

You will have carried out at least one practical within social psychology, which will have been either a questionnaire or an interview. Go back over your notes to revise what you did, as it is not possible here to help you to revise that part of the course.

Some general ideas about the practical and what to learn

Make sure you know about:

- qualitative and quantitative data and how you gathered both types of data
- the aims of your study
- how you drew up either the questionnaire or the interview schedule
- what type of sampling you used and why
- how to use techniques such as Likert-type questions to gather data
- what personal data are and why they are needed
- what is meant by standardised instructions and why they are important
- how to analyse quantitative data in terms of numbers and percentages, for example
- how to analyse qualitative data in terms of generating themes, for example

- ethical issues you addressed, and perhaps any ethical issues you could not address
- issues you controlled, such as how the questions were asked or having the same standardised instructions — and perhaps issues you could not control
- the independent variable, if there was one, such as whether someone was talking about their in-group or out-group or showing how they are agents of someone in authority
- the dependent variable, if there was one, is what was measured to show the concepts being studied (such as a score for preferring in-group members)
- conclusions that you drew, so that you can show that you fully understand what you found

Knowledge check 26

With regard to your practical in social psychology, explain your sampling technique (how did you find your participants?) and one way in which you dealt with an ethical guideline.

Summary

- Revise the practical that you carried out, as you will be asked information about what you did and what you found, for example.
- The practical must have used either a questionnaire or an interview.
- You must have gathered qualitative and quantitative data and be able to talk about both.
- Make sure that your work is ethical and that you can answer questions about the ethics of your work.
- Design decisions include the planning of the survey (e.g. standardised instructions, what questions are asked and reasons for choosing them), what ethical issues there are, considering a pilot study, thinking about any controls necessary and choosing the type of data (qualitative and quantitative), with reasons for your choice.
- Sampling decisions are important, including who the participants were and how they were found.
- Prepare an analysis of both the qualitative and quantitative data, as well as brief conclusions about the findings and the area of the study.

The cognitive approach

Unit 1 covers the social and the cognitive approaches. This section looks at the cognitive approach.

Table 28 Summary of the cognitive approach

Definition and key terms
The approach is defined in this section, and key terms are defined where they appear in the Content Guidance section.

Methodology
The main research method you will study within the cognitive approach is the experiment — laboratory, field and natural experiments — together with related terminology. Quite a few of the terms have been covered within the social approach and only the additional terms are explained in this section.

Content
Within cognitive psychology — which is a large field — you need to cover the levels of processing theory about memory and one other theory of memory. You also need to know about the cue-dependent theory of forgetting and one other theory of forgetting. Here the 'other' theory of memory chosen is reconstructive memory and the 'other' theory of forgetting is interference theory. Both are chosen because they will be useful for the key issue. If you studied a different 'other' theory for memory and/or forgetting, it is probably best to stick to the one you know.

Examiner tip

Look at past papers to see the format of questions about practicals in the AS part of the course. There is no guarantee that questions will always be in the same format but it would be a good idea to use your own practical for the social approach to prepare answers to questions that have already been asked. You can use the material in a different way if you need to, but preparation for such questions is useful.

Definition and key terms
Two studies in detail
You have to cover Godden and Baddeley's (1975) study of divers and whether they forgot more in the same context or when they recalled in a different context. As well as this 'set' study, you have to learn one other from Peterson and Peterson (1959), Craik and Tulving (1975) or Ramponi et al. (2004). Here Craik and Tulving (1975) is chosen because you need it to help you understand the levels of processing framework of how memory works. However, you might like to revise the study that you covered in your own course, if it was a different one.
One key issue
You will have studied a key issue in the cognitive approach and could revise that, but here the one chosen is the reliability of eyewitness testimony, so you could use that if you wish (if you studied a different issue).
Practical
It is best to use your own practical, as obviously a practical cannot be done here. A list is provided in this section to remind you of what you need to know for the exam.

Definition and key terms

Underpinning ideas (assumptions) about the cognitive approach and cognitive psychology

The cognitive approach is about the processing of information. If you think about information coming in through the senses (sight, hearing, smell, taste and touch), the cognitive approach is about what happens to the information then, including how it is processed in the brain and what the result of that processing is. The multi-store model (see Figure 1) is a theory of memory that shows clearly one idea of how information is processed in order to retain it (memory), and this model is an example of information processing. There is input, some processing occurs, and then there is output.

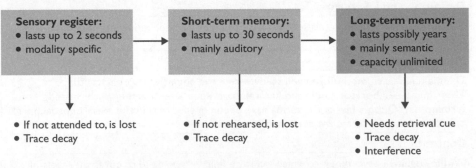

Figure 1 The multi-store model

The cognitive approach has also used the idea of the brain being like a computer — which has input, processing and output. Using the computer analogy (which is what comparing the brain to a computer is called), ideas can be suggested for how processing (in the form of perceiving, remembering, using language and forgetting) takes place. A model of memory called 'spreading activation' was developed, in part to try to understand how to programme a computer to understand language, for example.

Defining the terms

Terms that you need to be able to define for the cognitive approach are listed. A question will often ask 'What is meant by...?' and give the term. The terms are: **information processing**, **memory**, **storage**, **retrieval** and **forgetting**. In this section on cognitive psychology, you will find these terms defined (for example information processing, which has already been explained).

Summary

- The cognitive approach covers brain processing and nowadays would link to neuroscience and actual brain functioning, but as an early approach it is about modelling processes rather than the biological elements.
- Modelling is about working out the principles of processing and models. Includes the multi-store model of memory, reconstructive memory and cue-dependent forgetting.
- The computer analogy has been used to help understand cognitive processes — and the way the brain processes information can be used in computing too.
- Memory is part of cognitive psychology and looks at encoding, storage and recall processes.
- There are theories of forgetting too, such as that forgetting is about not having cues present to trigger memory.
- Terms to consider in cognitive psychology include information processing, memory, forgetting, storage and retrieval.

Methodology

What is explained here includes only what you need for the cognitive approach, in addition to what has already been explained within the social approach in the methodology section. First, it is worth considering what you might be asked about regarding the cognitive approach covered earlier in this book. The following table lists what you should already know from having revised the social approach.

Table 29 Cognitive approach as covered in this book

Feature of experiments	Tick if understood
Alternative hypothesis	
Independent variable (IV)	
Dependent variable (DV)	
Operationalisation	
Control	
Situational variables	
Participant variables	
Condition	
Objectivity/subjectivity	

Examiner tip

Use the idea of information processing and the idea of a computer analogy as two underpinning ideas within cognitive psychology and think of an example to show your understanding. Then list the five terms given here, and make sure you can say what is meant by each of them. This would give you a clear overview of the approach. An overview can be extremely useful when learning, as it helps you to put other material into context.

Knowledge check 27

Explain the term 'information processing'.

Examiner tip

The specification splits methodology up so that each approach includes some important methodological issues. However, this is rather artificial and in reality methodological issues will be repeated. Repetition aids recall, so the more you look again at methodological terms such as those listed here, the more you will understand them. So perhaps instead of looking at the terms and ticking that you understand them, practise explaining them to someone else (or imagine doing that).

Knowledge check 28

Give one example of a situational variable and one of a participant variable.

Examiner tip

The IV usually has two parts to it, reflecting two conditions of the study. In the example provided here, one group of participants was given words with a theme and the other group words with no theme. It is tempting perhaps to say that the IV is 'theme'. However, the IV is actually 'whether the words have a theme or not'. A good tip is not to give one-word answers for the IV.

Feature of experiments	Tick if understood
Reliability	
Validity	
Experimenter effects	
Demand characteristics	

There are other features of experiments that you need to know about. They are explained here.

Three types of experiment

There are three types of experiment — laboratory, field and natural experiments. It is rare to come across a natural experiment, but you will study both field and laboratory experiments and you need to know what a natural experiment is.

Laboratory experiments

- These are experiments carried out in an artificial controlled setting, such as a laboratory. The main feature is control and the setting is an unnatural one for the participants because of this control.
- The independent variable (IV) is manipulated in some way, usually using two conditions, sometimes more. For example, some participants could be asked to learn and recall a list of words that all had a similar theme. Another group of participants could be asked to learn and recall a list with the same number of words, of similar length, but this time a random list without a theme. There would be two conditions — whether the list had words with a theme (such as all colour words) or no theme (randomly chosen). The IV is whether words have a theme or not.
- The dependent variable (DV) is recorded, and in the example here the DV would be how many of the words in the list were recalled by each participant.
- Participant and situational variables would be controlled in a laboratory experiment, for example by using the same room at the same time of day (situational variables) and making sure as far as possible that participants were not hungry in one of the conditions and not the other, and so on (participant variables).
- The aim of a laboratory experiment is to find a cause and effect conclusion so that scientific knowledge can be built.

Field experiments

These are experiments carried out 'in the field', which means in the participants' natural setting. This can be, for example, a school (for teachers or pupils), a hospital (for doctors, nurses or patients) or a prison (for prisoners and guards). The main feature is the natural setting, together with the controls of a laboratory experiment, though these may be difficult to put into place.

Apart from the natural setting, field experiments have the same features as laboratory experiments, including IV, DV, controls and aiming for cause-and-effect conclusions.

Natural experiments

- These are experiments that tend to be 'in the field' because the independent variable occurs naturally. This is the main feature — that the IV is not something manipulated or set up, but is found already 'out there'.
- For example, when researchers wanted to see the effects of television on children, they studied a community where television was to be introduced. They studied the community beforehand and afterwards, and those were the two conditions of the IV. They did not introduce the television; it was being introduced in any case — it was a naturally occurring situation.
- Other independent variables (not only those in a natural setting) can be naturally occurring, such as gender. However, usually experiments using this sort of naturally occurring IV (such as gender rather than something in the natural setting) are called quasi-experiments because in other respects they are like laboratory experiments and can take place in a laboratory. Truly natural experiments tend to be 'in the field' and have a more complex IV (for example, the introduction of television is more complex than someone's gender).

Table 30 Strengths of the different types of experiment

Laboratory	Field	Natural
Good controls; replicable; reliability can be tested	More ecologically valid than laboratory experiments because they take place in natural settings	Independent variable occurs naturally, so valid because not artificially set up
Good controls; cause-and-effect relationship can be established	Fairly replicable because of experimental features	Tend to take place in a natural environment so likely to be ecologically valid

Table 31 Weaknesses of the different types of experiment

Laboratory	Field	Natural
So controlled that tasks may not give valid results because they are not natural/real	Natural setting, so hard to control all factors, which means results may be less valid	Difficult to control variables because the independent variable is naturally occurring, making it difficult to isolate all factors that might affect results
Environment unnatural and controlled, so not ecologically valid	Hard to control because of natural setting, so may not be replicable	Hard to control for experimenter effects; using a double-blind technique is not straightforward because most are carried out in natural settings
Experimenter effects can mean results are not valid because there may then be bias	Experimenter effects can mean results are not valid because there may then be bias	

Examiner tip

The DV is what is measured in a study and will be whatever the results are in a table or graph. In the example provided here, the researcher thinks more of the words will be recalled if there is a theme, and is measuring the number of words correctly recalled from the list, which is the DV. With the DV, also avoid one-word answers (such as 'recall').

Knowledge check 29

Give two differences and two similarities between a field experiment and a laboratory experiment.

Examiner tip

If revision time is short, it can be useful to focus on evaluation and to use it to draw out description points. For example, learning strengths and weaknesses of the different types of experiment can help in understanding what the three types are and describing them accurately (e.g. a weakness of a natural experiment is that it is hard to control variables because the independent variable is naturally occurring — this tells you what a natural experiment is).

Knowledge check 30

What are two strengths of the natural experiment as a research method?

Examiner tip

A question about a research method may seem ambiguous, so read the question carefully. For example, 'a natural experiment' in the question 'What is one strength of a natural experiment?' can imply 'the natural experiment as a research method' or 'a natural experiment that has been carried out'. Look for words that focus the question, for example 'as a research method' in Knowledge check 30.

Knowledge check 31

For each of the three designs, what is one study you could make up that the design could be used for and why?

Examiner tip

Tables that summarise strengths and weaknesses help revision. However, make sure that for each short summary point you are able to expand it fully to make it very clear. Take one or two of the points in the table here and write them out in sufficient detail that you could get 2 marks, for example.

Experimental (participant) designs

There are three **experimental designs**, sometimes called **participant designs** to remind you that they concern the participants in an experiment. There are only three ways of sorting participants into groups to study them.

- **Independent groups design** means to have different participants for each condition. Each group is independent of the other groups with regard to the people doing the study. If one group learns and recalls words that have colour meanings and a different group learns and recalls random words, this is an independent groups design.
- **Repeated measures design** means that all the conditions involve the same participants. For example, the person who learns and recalls the words that have colour meanings is also the person who learns and recalls the random words.
- **Matched pairs design** means different participants in the conditions, as in an independent groups design. But the participants are matched so that the two groups have 'as if' the same people. For example, if one participant is male, aged 20 and a student, there will be another 20-year-old male student in the other group.

Table 32 Strengths of the different participant designs

Repeated measures	Independent groups	Matched pairs
Participant variables are controlled because all participants do all conditions	No order effects to affect results	Helps to control participant variables
Uses fewer participants, so more efficient in terms of cost, convenience and ethics	Demand characteristics less likely	No order effects

Table 33 Weaknesses of the different participant designs

Repeated measures	Independent groups	Matched pairs
Order effects such as practice and fatigue effects can affect the results if there is no counterbalancing	Participant variables may affect the results	Different people are used, so there may be participant variables that affect the results
Demand characteristics are possible because participants could guess the aim(s) of the study	More participants are needed, so less efficient and less ethical	More participants are needed, so less efficient in terms of cost and less ethical

Experimental hypothesis (and whether directional or non-directional)

- In most studies there is a hypothesis (though there are exceptions, as in case studies, which you will study later in your course).
- A hypothesis is a statement of what is expected. So in the example that has been used in this section, it could be said that the hypothesis is, 'It is expected that more words from a list of words with colour meanings are going to be recalled than words from a list where the words are random.'

- There is a **null hypothesis**, which is the one that is tested and which you will learn more about in Unit 2. The null hypothesis is that there is no difference, as predicted (e.g. no difference in recall for the two lists).
- There is the **alternative hypothesis** — the alternative to the null — that there is a difference, as predicted.
- In an experiment, the alternative is the **experimental hypothesis**.

Hypotheses (predictions) can be directional or non-directional.

- A **directional hypothesis** means that the direction of the difference is predicted. So if a hypothesis says that the words from the 'colour words' list are better remembered than the words from the 'random' list, this is directional (one list is *better* remembered).
- A **non-directional hypothesis** is where the direction is not predicted. For example, if the experimental hypothesis is that there is a difference in the number of words recalled depending on whether a list is of 'colour' words or of random words, this does not give the direction.
- If we say boys are more aggressive than girls, we give direction (directional). If we say children differ in aggression according to gender, we don't give direction (non-directional).
- For information, because you will need to know in Unit 2 and also because of the way the questions might be asked, 'directional' is sometimes called 'one-tailed' and 'non-directional' is sometimes called 'two-tailed'.

Order effects, counterbalancing and randomisation

If different people are doing the different conditions (conditions are the parts of the study, e.g. there are words with colour meaning to learn and there are words of random meaning to learn — two conditions), they won't learn from doing one condition and so do another one better. In addition, they won't get tired and do a second condition worse. However, if the same people do all the conditions they may well get practised and get better, or get tired and get worse. These two situations are called **order effects**, as they are due to the order in which the conditions are carried out. If a participant does worse because he or she becomes tired, this is called a **fatigue effect**. If a participant does better because they are more practised, this is called a **practice effect**.

There are two ways of avoiding order effects. One is to **counterbalance**, which means alternating the order in which the participant does the conditions. The other way is called **randomisation**, which means randomly choosing the order in which the participant does the conditions, for example by tossing a coin.

Table 34 Order effects and how to deal with them

Order effect/issue	What it means
Practice effect	Having done one of the tasks (conditions), the participant does the next one better because of having had practice.
Fatigue effect	Having done one of the tasks (conditions), the participant does the next one less well because of being tired.

Knowledge check 32

Give a directional experimental hypothesis for a study looking at whether learning underwater affects recall underwater compared with on land.

Examiner tip

Methodology questions often involve knowing the IV and the DV, considering controls, knowing the experimental design of the study or giving a hypothesis (often specifically asked for as directional (one-tailed) or non-directional (two-tailed)). So be ready to answer such questions by making up a short study, or using past papers to do so, and then considering the methodological issues involved.

Knowledge check 33

What are two ways of avoiding order effects?

Examiner tip

The glossary includes many methodology terms. Work through it picking out the methodology terms, make a list and then check that you can define all the terms and use them. Index cards might be a good way of revising, with the methodological term on one side and explanations and examples on the other.

Order effect/issue	What it means
Counterbalancing	Alternating the order in which the tasks are presented, to counteract order effects. If the first participant does task A then task B, the next does task B then task A. There would perhaps still be order effects but they would cancel each other out.
Randomisation	Choosing at random which task the participant will do first. This can be done by tossing a coin (e.g. heads it is task A first).

Summary

- There are three types of experiment: field, laboratory and natural.
- Experiments have an independent variable and a dependent variable.
- The IV and the DV must be carefully operationalised (they need to be made measurable).
- An experimental hypothesis is a statement of what is expected and can be directional (e.g. says which condition is better or worse) or non-directional (says there will be a difference but not in which direction).
- There are three experimental designs: repeated measures, independent groups and matched pairs.
- Experiments have careful controls to rule out participant and situational variables as well as experimenter effects and demand characteristics.
- Bias is more contained if there are no order effects and if conditions are either counterbalanced or randomised.
- Results are displayed using measures of central tendency (averages), measures of dispersion (e.g. range) and graphs (including bar graph, histogram and frequency graph).
- Issues around claiming that results are secure include objectivity (subjectivity and interpretation bring bias), validity (findings must relate to real life) and reliability (a study has to be shown to get the same results no matter how often the study is done).

Examiner tip

Studies are where researchers have formulated a hypothesis from theory and then collected data. Theories are ideas about how something works and they suggest that certain things might happen. Hypotheses are tighter statements about what might happen and they are then tested in a study to see what is found. Godden and Baddeley (1975) did a study where their hypothesis comes from the cue-dependent theory. Cue-dependent is the theory, Godden and Baddeley is the study.

Content

The content for cognitive psychology that you need to cover is clear: two models or theories of memory and two models or theories of forgetting. Four theories are explained briefly here. Some explanations are called theories, some are called models and one mentioned here is called a framework. It is hard to be precise about the differences between theory, model and framework, but this table gives suggestions about the differences.

Table 35 Theory, model and framework

Term	'What is meant by...'
Theory	Can be tested and predicts what will happen. A hypothesis is taken from a theory and then tested. If the hypothesis is supported by evidence, the theory continues; if not, it is amended or replaced.
Model	Involves generating an abstract idea of how something might happen and is not a theory until it is made testable against reality.
Framework	Suggests an idea or thought that is not firmed up enough (yet) to be a model or a theory ready to be tested.

Two theories/models of memory

The levels of processing framework and the reconstruction theory of memory are the two explained here. Memory is defined as taking in information that is then available for use later on, and is often said to have three stages — encoding, storage and retrieval. Information has to be encoded, which means memories are laid down in some way, and this is a physical trace in the brain. As well as encoding, the memory has to be stored, otherwise if the trace is lost, the information will have been forgotten. Storage is retaining the memory and keeping it in some way. If we are to remember something, that information has to be retrieved, which means getting the information back when required.

The key terms you need to be able to define for cognitive psychology are **information processing**, **memory**, **storage**, **retrieval** and **forgetting**. Forgetting is defined later in this section, and information processing (input, processing and output) was explained at the start of the material on cognitive psychology (see page 36). Here memory, storage and retrieval are explained. Make sure you can say what is meant by all five of these terms.

Levels of processing framework (LOP)

The levels of processing framework is an idea of how memory might occur. Information is processed at different levels, such as deeply attended to or less deeply attended to. Remembering information is about how deeply it is processed, rather than memory being 'something' in itself. According to this framework there are three levels of processing.

Table 36 Three levels of processing according to LOP

Level	Explanation
Structural (sight)	Processing at a structural level is seeing what something is like, e.g. with words, whether there are capital letters or lower case (i.e. TABLE or table), or how many letters go below the line (e.g. 'y', 'g').
Phonemic (sound)	Processing phonemically means considering how something sounds, e.g. with words, whether one word rhymes with another (e.g. cat, mat) or not (e.g. cat, dog).
Semantic (meaning)	Processing semantically means considering the meaning of something, e.g. with words, what the word means. For example, whether a word fits in a sentence (e.g. cat: 'the cat has smooth fur' compared with table: 'the table has smooth fur').

According to this framework, memory comes from depth of processing. If there is no depth of processing — such as when no attention at all is paid to something — there is no memory trace. If there is shallow processing — such as structural processing — there is not a strong memory trace. However, if there is deep processing — such as when meaning is considered — there is a stronger memory trace.

Craik and Tulving's (1975) study explains the levels of processing idea and is described in the 'Two studies in detail' section on pages 49–51.

Knowledge check 34

If asked to describe a theory of forgetting, is it right to describe Godden and Baddeley's (1975) study? What would be a right answer?

Examiner tip

Definitions can be in multiple-choice format. You can be asked which of a choice of four (usually) is the best definition of a term. Two strategies: 1) think of the answer before you look at the choices — it is less likely that one of the choices will persuade you (wrongly); 2) rule out those you know are wrong, leaving you with fewer choices.

Examiner tip

Always read exam questions several times. There is a danger in seeing a term and jumping to conclusions about the question, or in getting names and theories or studies confused. For example, a *study* looking into levels of processing is Craik and Tulving's. A *theory* that suggests memory is about levels of processing is Craik and *Lockhart*'s theory that deeper processing leads to better recall. Your answer must match the question.

Knowledge check 35

What are the three levels of processing and which leads to the best recall?

Table 37 Strengths and weaknesses of the levels-of-processing framework

Strengths	Weaknesses
There is evidence for the framework: Hyde and Jenkins (1971) and Craik and Tulving (1975).	Depth of processing also tends to mean more time spent processing; it might be that the time spent makes the memory stronger, not the depth of processing.
It links research into memory with research into perception and selective attention; it focuses on information processing and the whole process; this means it is a stronger explanation than the multi-store model, because more studies can be explained by it.	There may be more effort involved in 'deeper' processing and the greater effort might account for the better recall; the term 'deep' is not well defined by Craik and Lockhart (1972); it could be time spent processing, effort involved or using past experiences and adding meaning.

Reconstructive memory

Bartlett was a well-known psychologist working as long ago as 1932 and he developed a theory that is still used and respected today. He made famous the idea that memory is not a completely accurate recording of what happens in life. He put forward the idea that we use our past experiences when recording current events and laying down memories. He said we have schemata (plural of schema) — which are plans and information about things that we have already learned or assumed. For example, you have a schema for eating in a restaurant — you know that you have to order, and that you have to pay at the end, and that you use a knife and fork, and so on. We process information through these schemata without knowing it, and this means our memories are affected and what we recall is not 'pure' information. 'Remembering' is not just playing back a video recording as we would from a mobile phone — it is using what was seen or heard and relating the story which is filtered through past experiences and schemata. This means that memory is reconstructed.

Bartlett (1932) ran a famous experiment to illustrate his theory of reconstruction. He read participants a story called *The War of the Ghosts*, which was a story from a different culture that did not make sense easily, so the participants did not have a schema for all the events in the story. He found a number of features in the recall of the story. He found that participants added to the story so that it made sense to them, which he called confabulation. They altered some important parts to fit their own schemata too, which he called rationalisation. For example, the story ends with someone 'falling down dead' at sunrise, whereas people tended to say it was at sunset as that fitted better for them. He found that participants picked out central features (to them) of the story and missed out other bits — usually what did not make sense to them. And when he asked them to remember it again, after a short while, they recalled less. Using this story, he showed that people reconstructed the story so that it made sense and to fit their schemata.

Table 38 Strengths and weaknesses of the theory of reconstructive memory

Strengths	Weaknesses
There is much evidence for the theory: Bartlett (1932) and the work of Loftus on eyewitness testimony	Bartlett's (1932) story did not make sense so participants may have altered it because of demand characteristics
The theory can be tested experimentally	The theory describes memory as reconstructive but does not deal with the processes

Table 39 Comparisons between levels of processing and reconstruction theory

Levels of processing framework	Theory of reconstructive memory
Used laboratory experiments when testing — using lists of words	Used experiments when testing — using stories
Suggests memory is not a thing but just part of processing information, and only occurs when information is processed quite deeply	Suggests memory is something to study on its own, that is part of processing information but not 'just' a by-product of processing as suggested by LOP
Looks at three levels of processing, including using meaning	Looks at the effects of previous experiences and schemata on recall
Has a useful application in revision and studying as well as in helping recall — it is known that to remember you need to add meaning	Has a useful application in the legal system because eyewitness testimony can be taken as absolute, but the theory suggests it is not like a tape recording and is affected by previous experience

Two theories/models of forgetting

The cue-dependent and interference theory of forgetting are the two explained here. One point about memory and forgetting is worth taking note of. In your course, when you are writing about forgetting, try to focus on that and not on remembering. For example, when discussing the reconstructive elements of memory you might want to talk about forgetting material that does not 'fit' — but try to focus on memory being altered by schemata and not on what is forgotten. Similarly, with cue-dependent forgetting, you will see that you could talk about cues helping us to remember, but try to focus on lack of cues leading us to forget.

Cue-dependent forgetting

Cue-dependent forgetting theory was put forward by Tulving (1975), who suggested that the absence of cues leads to forgetting. Tulving defined forgetting as 'the inability to recall something now that could be recalled on an earlier occasion'. Cues are things in the environment that were present when the memory was encoded — and Tulving was talking about the cognitive environment. Such cues are called retrieval cues. The cognitive environment is what is around both externally and internally when memories are encoded, so those features are encoded too, or at least affect encoding. Encoding means laying down memories. Forgetting occurs, according to the cue-dependent theory of forgetting, when the cognitive environment is different from what it was when a memory was encoded. It follows that forgetting is reduced if the cognitive environment is reinstated.

Examiner tip

Make use of your own understanding of memory when revising. Use poems, summaries, letters of words as acronyms etc. Add meaning to the material as much as possible to aid your recall. For example, SPAM might help you to remember the levels of processing: structural, phonemic and semantic, or SPandS (make up your own — it adds more meaning for you).

Knowledge check 37

With regard to your situation at this moment in time, and thinking what would help later recall, state one state-dependent cue and one context-dependent cue (see page 46).

Examiner tip

When describing a theory such as cue-dependent theory, i.e. where there are parts to the theory, take care to explain the parts fully. It is not likely that mentioning 'state-dependent cues' and 'context-dependent cues' will get a mark each unless there is elaboration. Lists in an answer tend to get just 1 mark, so make sure you know enough about each part to explain a little and give an example (a useful way of showing understanding).

Knowledge check 38

Briefly outline what it means to say that 'forgetting is less if the cognitive environment is reinstated'.

Two types of cue are discussed in the theory of cue-dependent forgetting. There are cues — state-dependent cues — that depend on the emotional state of the individual or their physical state, such as hunger or tiredness. There are cues that depend on the context someone is in — context-dependent cues — such as their actual environment (where they are) and things around them. The theory suggests that there is state-dependent forgetting, because the person is not in the same state as they were when memories were encoded. In addition, there is context-dependent forgetting, which occurs because the person is not in the same situation as when the memories were encoded.

Godden and Baddeley's (1975) field experiment studied cue-dependent forgetting and is explained in the section that follows, looking at two studies in detail. Use evidence from their study to help to describe and evaluate the cue-dependent theory of forgetting.

Table 40 Strengths and weaknesses of the cue-dependent theory of forgetting

Strengths	Weaknesses
This theory accounts for forgetting in different tasks. There are many supporting studies	Tasks are artificial, so the results might lack validity
The idea is testable because the retrieval environment can be replicated	It may only account for some forms of forgetting

The interference theory of forgetting

Interference theory suggests that forgetting occurs because some information interferes with other information. Memory is often split into short-term memory, which lasts up to 30 seconds and holds a limited amount of information, and long-term memory, which potentially lasts a lifetime and holds an unlimited amount of information. In short-term memory, interference causes forgetting when some information prevents other information from being encoded into long-term memory. The interference theory of forgetting also looks at forgetting in long-term memory. The idea is that information already stored in long-term memory can get in the way of encoding and storing new information. Another way that interference causes forgetting is that new information can interfere with what is already stored.

Table 41 Two types of interference causing forgetting in long-term memory

Type of interference	Explanation	Example
Retroactive interference	Material that is learned now gets in the way of (interferes with) material that has been previously stored, so retrieval is affected (there is forgetting).	Learning French now gets in the way of previously learned Spanish (you remember the French word but have now forgotten the Spanish word that you knew before).
Proactive interference	Material that was learned in the past gets in the way of (interferes with) material that is being stored now, so retrieval is affected (there is forgetting).	Learned Spanish — words you already know — gets in the way of learning French now (you remember the Spanish word but that gets in the way of you remembering the French word).

Table 42 Strengths and weaknesses of the interference theory of forgetting

Strengths	Weaknesses
There is much evidence to support the theory, e.g. Jenkins and Dallenbach (1924)	It is hard to separate interference from displacement and trace decay; it can be shown that interference seems to happen but not why this happens or what occurs
It has been tested by experiment, giving cause-and-effect relationships. Experiments have been replicated and appear to be reliable	Tasks used in experiments are artificial and may lack validity

Table 43 Comparing two theories of forgetting

Cue-dependent theory of forgetting	Interference theory of forgetting
Used laboratory experiments to test the theory, which can lack validity because of artificial tasks	Used laboratory experiments to test the theory, which can lack validity because of artificial tasks
Considers what was in the environment and how not reproducing that would cause forgetting (prevent retrieval)	Considers what is already stored in long-term memory and how that would affect storage of new material
The theory considers how encoding affects storage (the theory includes cues and how material is stored), which would affect retrieval	The theory considers how storage (what was stored) would affect retrieval
Suggests that reinstating the cognitive environment (cues) would help stop forgetting	Seems to suggest that forgetting is inevitable if material is similar

Examiner tip

It is useful to think of questions as testing your 'knowledge *with understanding*' rather than just your 'knowledge' (e.g. rote-learned). Show understanding throughout all your answers, adding relevant examples whenever you can.

Knowledge check 39

The strengths and weaknesses here are brief. Explain in detail one strength and one weakness of interference as a theory of forgetting.

- The levels of processing framework (LOP) for memory suggests that we remember more when we process more deeply, which is semantic processing.
- LOP puts forward three levels of processing: structural (what we see), phonemic (what we hear) and semantic (adding meaning).
- Craik and Tulving (1975) carried out a study that showed that semantic processing did indeed lead to better recall and also took longer, so this backed up the LOP framework.
- Reconstructive memory is another theory, linked to Alan Baddeley, and the theory suggests that memory is not like a recording, it is reconstructed (and so not faithful to reality).
- Baddeley carried out a study using the *War of the Ghosts* story and showed that when people did not have clear schemas for what was being encoded, they changed bits to suit their own schemas (rationalisation).

- Reconstructive memory is a useful theory to refer to when explaining how an eyewitness is not likely to give a completely accurate (as if recorded) account of what they see.
- Cue-dependent forgetting suggests that we forget if the cues that were present when the encoding took place are not present at recall.
- Cues include context-dependent cues (the environment at the time) and state-dependent cues (the person's feelings and 'state' at the time).
- Godden and Baddeley (1975) found evidence of context-dependent cues being important because divers recalled more words when they recalled in the same context as when they learned the words.
- Another theory of forgetting is interference theory, which suggests that in short-term memory interfering with rehearsal processes can lead to no encoding (which is a type of forgetting) and also that in long-term memory one set of learning might interfere with another set of learning.

Summary

Examiner tip

You can compare theories by looking at the methods used that give evidence for the theories, by studying their application to real-life situations and by considering basic ideas of the theories themselves. You can look at similarities and differences in strengths or weaknesses. Make a revision list, e.g. using URVAR: underpinning ideas, research method, validity, application, reliability.

Knowledge check 40

What is the research method that Godden and Baddeley used in their 1975 study?

Examiner tip

Prepare for questions that not only ask you to describe the complete study, but also ask for specific parts of a study such as just the procedure (or just the findings, which would be 'results and/or conclusions'). This means that you need sufficient detail of the parts (aims, procedure, results, conclusions) to answer a question on just one of them.

Two studies in detail

The two studies in detail explained here are Godden and Baddeley's (1975) study of divers and how context affects forgetting, and Craik and Tulving's (1975) study of levels of processing. Godden and Baddeley's study helps to describe and evaluate the cue-dependent theory of forgetting, and it is a compulsory study, so you have to know it in detail. Craik and Tulving's study helps to describe and evaluate the levels of processing framework for explaining memory and it is a choice in your course. If you have studied either Peterson and Peterson (1959) or Ramponi et al. (2004) instead, you could revise that study instead of learning Craik and Tulving.

Godden and Baddeley's (1975) study of divers

Aims

Godden and Baddeley wanted to study the effect of environment on recall and the effect of retrieval cues. They aimed to look at context cues rather than state cues. Their specific aim was to see if there was better recall when the recall environment was the same as the learning environment. They chose two natural environments and the two environments were clearly different, so that the contexts were clearly different. They wanted to have a valid study, so they used naturally occurring environments and did a field study.

Procedure

- Godden and Baddeley chose divers as their participants. There were 13 male and five female participants, who were all members of a diving club. They were on a diving holiday in Scotland.
- They chose 'underwater' as one environment and 'on land' as the other environment.
- The same divers had to learn a list of words either on land ('dry') or underwater ('wet'). Then they had to recall the words either on land ('dry') or underwater ('wet'). There were 36 words of two or three syllables, randomly chosen.
- So there were four conditions:
  – 'dry' learning and 'dry' recall   – 'wet' learning and 'wet' recall
  – 'dry' learning and 'wet' recall   – 'wet' learning and 'dry' recall
- The first two ('dry' and 'dry' and 'wet' and 'wet') were where the retrieval cues were the same as the cues at encoding and storage.
- The second two ('dry' and 'wet' and 'wet' and 'dry') were where the cues at encoding and storage were not present as retrieval cues for recall.
- The hypothesis was that divers would remember more words (forget less) if the learning and recall environments were the same (either learning and recalling underwater or learning and recalling on land) than if the learning and recall environments were different (either learning underwater and recalling on land or learning on land and recalling underwater).
- The independent variable is whether the two contexts (environments) are the same or different.
- The dependent variable was how many words are correctly recalled.
- The same divers did all four conditions, so this was a repeated measures design.

Results

Table 44 Percentage of words recalled out of 36 words depending on the learning and recall contexts

Learning environment	Recall environment dry	Recall environment wet
Dry	37	24
Wet	23	32

The table shows that the percentages were higher when the learning environment and the recall environment were the same (37% and 32%). When the learning environment and recall environment were different, recall was lower (23% and 24%).

Conclusions

Context is a retrieval cue, and when the cognitive environment at recall is the same as at encoding, forgetting is less.

Table 45 Strengths and weaknesses of the Godden and Baddeley (1975) study

Strengths	Weaknesses
It was an experiment with clear controls, so replicable; this means it can be tested for reliability and is a scientific study	The situation was artificial and the contexts were very different; this means the results may not be valid
The environment was familiar to the participants, who were divers, so there was some ecological validity	The results showed a lot of forgetting even when the context for encoding and recall were the same; therefore, context dependency cannot be the only reason for forgetting

Craik and Tulving's (1975) study of levels of processing

Aims

The main aim of Craik and Tulving's (1975) study was to test the levels of processing (LOP) framework. They wanted to see if structural processing led to low recall, phonemic processing led to better recall and semantic processing led to the best recall, which is what LOP suggests. When they talked about better recall they meant that the memory trace was durable — it would fade most quickly when material was structurally processed and least quickly with semantic processing. They also wanted to see if semantic processing meant processing for a longer time.

Procedure

- They operationalised shallow processing by asking participants to consider the structure of words, such as whether the word is in upper or lower case letters.
- They operationalised intermediate processing by asking participants to consider whether a word rhymed with another word or not, which is phonemic processing.
- They operationalised deep processing by asking participants to answer questions based on considering the meaning of a word, which is semantic processing.

Examiner tip
When giving the results of a study, where possible give the actual figures. This is a 'study in detail' so details are expected.

Examiner tip
For marking purposes, a study is divided into aim, procedure, results and conclusions (APRC) because it is felt that when describing the study, missing out results or conclusions, or missing out aims or procedure, means that the study is not understood sufficiently. So when describing a study, aim to include at least three of the four elements, so that you give enough to make the whole study understandable. Marking will reflect these four 'parts'.

Knowledge check 41
Explain why Godden and Baddeley's (1975) study is an experiment.

Examiner tip
Many studies have more than one aim, so in an exam answer make sure to mention more than one aim if there are several. Revise two aims for each study if possible, as that will add depth to your answer and will help your understanding and recall of the study.

- Participants were tested individually. Words were flashed up on a screen in front of the participant after a question had been asked. The questions required either structural processing, phonemic processing or semantic processing. After the word was quickly flashed in front of them, the participant had to press 'yes' or 'no' as their answer. The questions were set up so that the numbers requiring 'yes' and 'no' answers were even.
- All participants did all the questions, so this was a repeated measures design.
- After all the questions had been answered, the participants were given an unexpected recognition or recall task. There were a number of experiments with slightly different procedures, but the procedure given here is the basic one. For example, for one experiment 40 questions were asked, so 40 words were used in the test condition; then the recognition task used 80 words and the participants had to say whether the words had been part of the task or not.

Results

In one experiment Craik and Tulving asked five different questions which required 'yes' or 'no' responses. The results of asking these five questions, with the proportion of the words correctly recognised and the time it took to reply, are given here.

Table 46 Time taken to answer 'yes' or 'no' to the five questions

Response time in milliseconds	Level of processing from shallow (1) to deepest (5)				
	(1) Is there a word?	**(2) Is the word in capital letters?**	**(3) Does the word rhyme?**	**(4) Does the word fit the category?**	**(5) Does the word fit the sentence?**
Yes	591	614	689	711	741
No	590	625	678	716	832

It can be seen that the more the question required thinking about (more depth of processing, perhaps), the longer it took for the participant to press either 'yes' or 'no'. This was true both for 'yes' and 'no' answers. It took a little longer to respond to 'no' questions when thinking about whether a word fitted a sentence, but for the other levels, whether the answer was 'yes' or 'no' made little difference to the time.

Table 47 Proportion of words recognised correctly for answers 'yes' or 'no' to the five questions

Proportion of words recognised correctly	Level of processing from shallow (1) to deepest (5)				
	(1) Is there a word?	**(2) Is the word in capital letters?**	**(3) Does the word rhyme?**	**(4) Does the word fit the category?**	**(5) Does the word fit the sentence?**
Yes	0.22	0.18	0.78	0.93	0.96
No	N/A	0.14	0.36	0.63	0.83

The first two questions (whether there is a word and whether the word is in capital letters) can both be considered as structural processing, and the last two questions can both be considered as needing semantic processing. Looking at the questions as having three depths (1 + 2, 3, 4 + 5), it is clear that the proportion of words recognised correctly depends on the depth of processing, with structural processing giving the least recognition, graduating to phonemic processing, and semantic processing giving the most recognition. This was the case for both 'yes' and 'no' answers. When a word rhymed, however (a 'yes' answer), there was a much better recognition rate than if the word did not rhyme (a 'no' answer), which you might think is because the meaning of the word was then better recorded.

Conclusions

Craik and Tulving's study backs up the LOP idea and shows that semantic processing leads to the best recall and also takes longer. It could be that depth of processing leads to better recall, or that length of processing leads to better recall, or some combination of these issues.

Table 48 Strengths and weaknesses of the study by Craik and Tulving (1975)

Strengths	Weaknesses
The experiments were controlled carefully, so the study is replicable; replication occurred within the study so the findings are reliable	Even if 'deeper' means longer processing, it might still be that the improved recognition is due to the length of processing time, not the depth of processing
The study reinforces the levels of processing framework; the study looks at depth meaning longer processing time	The tasks are artificial, so the study could lack validity

Table 49 Comparisons between the two studies

Godden and Baddeley (1975)	Craik and Tulving (1975)
An experimental study carried out in 1975, using careful controls to look for cause and effect links	An experimental study carried out in 1975 using careful controls to look for cause and effect links
A field experiment that can claim ecological validity to an extent because it used divers in their natural environment	A laboratory experiment that loses out on ecological validity as the setting was not natural for processing meaning in everyday life
Uses words to test recall, which may not be valid because there is a lot more to memory than learning words	Uses words to test recall, which may not be valid because there is a lot more to memory than learning words
Gives clear evidence to back the theory of cue-dependent forgetting, showing that the context where learning takes place helps recall	Gives clear evidence to back the theory of levels of processing, showing that the deeper the processing the better the recall

Knowledge check 42

Give four 'results' of Craik and Tulving's (1975) study.

Examiner tip

Evaluate studies as precisely as you can. For example, referring to Craik and Tulving, 'This was a lab experiment so had careful controls and was reliable' may be true but the question is not asking for an evaluation of lab experiments. Instead, write: 'This was a lab experiment so had careful controls, such as keeping the items and questions the same for all participants, so the study could be repeated and tested for reliability, which is a strength.'

Summary

- The compulsory study in detail for the cognitive approach is Godden and Baddeley's (1975) study, which looks at cue-dependent forgetting, focusing on context dependency.
- Godden and Baddeley (1975) found evidence for context-dependent forgetting because recall was better when in the same context as learning, whether learning and recall were both on land or whether they were both underwater.
- Another of the studies for this section is Craik and Tulving (1975) (there are two others that could be chosen).
- Craik and Tulving found that the deeper the processing (needing to add meaning), the better the recall of words, which reinforced the LOP framework of memory.
- As both Godden and Baddeley (1975) and Craik and Tulving (1975) used experimental methods, both of their studies could be said to lack validity because of the tight controls. However, Godden and Baddeley used real divers in their natural diving setting, so perhaps they could claim ecological validity, unlike Craik and Tulving (1975).

One key issue

Examiner tip

When asked to describe the issue, make sure that it is the issue (the problem, the debate) that you are describing and not the psychology explaining the issue. The issue here is not 'eyewitness testimony' as such; it is the problem with eyewitness testimony regarding its reliability, or the debate about how far it should be relied upon.

The key issue chosen is whether eyewitness testimony is reliable or not, and what the consequences are if it is unreliable. Eyewitness testimony is the statement given by someone who has seen an accident or crime — usually to the police — to say what they have seen. People can then give evidence in a court to say what they have seen, which is also eyewitness testimony. An eyewitness can be asked to pick someone out of a line-up, help to draw up an identikit picture of someone, or identify them in some other way. The point is that in general, it is thought that an eyewitness will be able to identify a suspect and give a good account of a situation. In practice, however, it seems that eyewitnesses can be unreliable. There are cases where someone has been imprisoned because of eyewitness testimony and then later it has been found that the person was not guilty. The issue is that eyewitness testimony appears to be unreliable.

Cognitive psychology can explain why eyewitness testimony is likely to be unreliable. One explanation is to consider the role of schemata in memory, as proposed by Bartlett (1932). Bartlett suggested that memory is not like a tape recorder, but instead involves amending material to ensure it makes sense and fits our schemata. There is likely to be confabulation, where someone will add to memory so that it makes sense. There is also rationalisation, which means features will be forgotten, again to make sense of what the eyewitness has seen. This uses the reconstruction theory of memory.

Elizabeth Loftus carried out many studies on the unreliability of eyewitness testimony, including a study by Loftus and Palmer (1975), which showed that when a verb in a question was changed, it affected the response to a question. When Loftus and Palmer asked about the speed of a car that 'smashed', 'hit' or 'collided with' (and other verbs) another car, the estimate of speed was higher for 'smashed' — presumably because it suggests the car was going faster. This suggests that leading questions guide eyewitness testimony. Another study showed that if an eyewitness was asked about 'a' broken headlight, there was less recall of broken glass than if they were asked about 'the' broken headlight, again showing the strength of leading questions.

On the other hand, Loftus also found later that only fairly unimportant information is affected by such leading questions — very important information seems less affected by how a question is worded. Nevertheless, Loftus found that if participants in a study were told there was an eyewitness to an incident, they were much more likely to believe the eyewitness, even if without that testimony there was not enough evidence for them to be so confident. It seems that juries believe eyewitnesses, even though their testimony is likely to be unreliable. Loftus and Ketcham (1991) suggested that eyewitness testimony might be responsible for an incorrect verdict about half of the time.

Knowledge check 43

Using concepts from cognitive psychology, explain how you would suggest improving revision techniques.

Summary

- The key issue discussed here is whether eyewitness testimony is as reliable as we would want, given the seriousness of the way it can be used (for example, causing someone to be imprisoned).

- Reconstructive memory theory suggests that we are likely to use our own schemata in a situation to encode memories and to recall, so eyewitness memory is not likely to be a complete recording of events — indeed is most *un*likely to be that.

- However, reconstructing the whole incident can be useful as it can reinstate context and possibly state-dependent cues to trigger recall, as suggested by the cue-dependent theory of forgetting, which is backed by Godden and Baddeley's (1975) field experiment.

- The cognitive interview is a technique used by police following findings from studies in the area of cognitive psychology, because in such an interview the person is not given leading questions, as Loftus in a variety of studies found that leading questions can affect recall (so that it is not accurate).

- The cognitive interview also involves bringing back state-dependent cues by asking the person to think back to the time to take themselves back into the 'state' they were in. The context can also be reinstated for them by means of a reconstruction or mentally.

- Another key issue that cognitive psychology can help with is learning techniques such as revision, because levels of processing theory, for example, suggests that recall is better if material is deeply processed (which means adding meaning), so the advice is to revise using different techniques and actively.

Practical

You will have carried out at least one practical within cognitive psychology, which will have been an experiment. Go back over your notes to revise what you did, as it is not possible here to help you to revise that part of the course.

Some general ideas about the practical and what to learn

Make sure you know about:
- the aim(s) of the practical
- the purpose of using the type of experiment you used (e.g. laboratory, field)
- your experimental hypothesis and null hypothesis
- the independent and dependent variable (fully operationalised)
- whether the hypothesis is directional or non-directional
- the participant design and why you chose that design

Examiner tip
Be ready for an issue to which you have to apply concepts from the approach. One idea might be the issue of helping someone to revise for an exam (focus on depth of processing or reinstating the context or state). Another idea is considering how to get more accurate eyewitness testimony from a witness (avoid leading questions or allow them to recall without guiding them). Practise using the ideas you have learned from cognitive psychology to explain such issues.

- the sampling method, why you chose it and what other method you might have chosen
- ethical issues and how they were dealt with
- ethical issues which should have been dealt with more fully
- the apparatus and why you chose it (e.g. why you chose those words, if applicable)
- whether you used counterbalancing and what you did about order effects (if you used repeated measures)
- what controls you put into place and why — and what was not controlled
- two problems with your study, apart from ethical issues and controls
- possible issues with regard to experimenter effects
- strengths of your study — considering issues such as validity, reliability, generalisability, objectivity and credibility
- which descriptive statistics you used (mean, median, mode, range, graphs) and why
- what the range means and why it is important
- how to draw and interpret a frequency graph

Summary

- The practical has to be an experiment and has to include aspects covered in the material specified for the cognitive approach.
- Ethical principles must be followed.
- Research design decisions are important in experiments (as in other research methods), such as the experimental design itself, decisions of how to control participant and situational variables, decisions about manipulation of the IV and decisions about how to measure the DV.
- The results must be analysed using measures of central tendency (mean, median and mode, as appropriate) and dispersion (range at least).
- Bar charts, histograms and frequency graphs are on the specification.
- The data are to be commented on as well, which can include evaluation of your study.

Questions & Answers

Examination structure and skills

Two approaches, six areas within each

The Unit 1 exam consists of questions split into three different types, ranging across the two approaches (the social approach and the cognitive approach). The three different types of question are multiple choice, short answer and extended answer questions. You will not know how many marks there are for each approach, but it is certain that both the Unit 1 approaches will be covered somewhere in the paper.

Within each approach there are six areas:
- key terms and the basics of the approach (definitions)
- methodology
- content
- two studies in detail
- a key issue
- a practical

The aim in the Unit 1 examination is to ask questions covering the six areas within the approaches, as well as the two approaches themselves. For example, if you are asked a question about a key issue in the cognitive approach, you are unlikely to be asked a 'key issue' question for the social approach in the same examination. You need to be prepared to answer a question on any of the six main areas for each of the two approaches.

Exam structure and assessment objectives (AOs)

Each of the two AS exam papers has multiple choice questions at the start, followed by some short answer questions, some extended writing questions and a 12-mark extended writing question (essay question) at the end.

The assessment objectives (AOs) of the AS exam papers are explained more fully below but can be briefly described as:
- **AO1** — testing knowledge with understanding and good communication skills
- **AO2** — testing evaluation, assessment and applications
- **AO3** — testing understanding and evaluation of methodology, including other people's studies

Don't think that someone sets each paper with past papers in front of them, avoiding what has been asked before. Imagine someone trying to set an interesting paper, covering the six areas, ranging across the approaches and balancing AO1, AO2 and AO3 marks according to the required percentages of each.

It is not possible to guess what will be on the paper — don't try. Prepare answers for all possible questions. The only guarantee is that there will be the three types of question (multiple choice, short answer and extended writing) and a 12-mark essay question at the end of each paper.

Different people set the papers, and there are not as many strict rules as you might think. Tips in this guide include words such as 'usually'. Each paper will be different and you have to be prepared to answer whatever questions appear. For example, there are many ways that short answer questions can be written, such as:

- 'Explain what is meant by...'
- 'Describe the procedure of...'
- 'Outline the theory...'
- 'Outline two weaknesses of...'
- 'What is the hypothesis in this study...?'

Read the question carefully and do what is asked, and you will do well.

The examination paper will be testing you according to assessment objectives (AOs), which concern the skills you need to show. These include what you know and understand (AO1), comments about what you know and understand, such as criticism (AO2) and knowledge and comments about methodological issues (AO3).

Assessment objectives

The assessment objectives are listed in the specification. A brief explanation is given below, but check the full list of what you will be assessed on.

Assessment objective 1: knowledge and understanding (AO1)

- You need to recognise, recall and show understanding of psychological knowledge, including theories, studies, methods and concepts, as well as psychological principles, perspectives and applications.
- You must communicate clearly and effectively, presenting and selecting material well. For example, if you are asked to explain what is meant by obedience for 3 marks and you just say that it is about obeying, you have not explained anything. You need to make your points clearly — for example:

'Obedience is about following the orders of someone in authority and can be explained by saying that someone is in an agentic state when they follow such orders. An example might be the obedience shown in Milgram's main study, when participants thought they were giving someone electric shocks and they continued, even though it clearly distressed them.'

- You may lose marks by using bullet points, so avoid them. The problem with bullet points is that they encourage shorthand, meaning that your answer will not be clearly and effectively communicated.

Assessment objective 2: evaluation and comment (AO2)

You must be able to:

- analyse and evaluate psychological theories and concepts, referring to relevant evidence
- apply psychological knowledge and understanding to unfamiliar situations
- assess the validity, reliability and credibility of psychological knowledge

Assessment objective 3: understanding and evaluation of methodology (AO3)

You must be able to:

- describe ethical, safe and skilful practical techniques and processes, including selecting appropriate qualitative and quantitative methods
- know how to make, record and communicate reliable and valid measurement, using primary and secondary sources
- analyse, explain, interpret and evaluate the methodology, results and impact of both your own practicals and the studies of others

The Unit 1 exam

Unit 1 is assessed in an 80-minute exam. Answers are written in a booklet similar to those used at GCSE. 60 marks are available. This means you need to score around 1 mark per minute, with 20 minutes to spare for reading and thinking. In general, you can expect to gain 1 mark for each point that answers the question, or for elaboration of a point.

Answers must be communicated 'clearly and effectively' (see AO1 above). Avoid one-word answers unless they are asked for.

The final essay question is usually worth 12 marks.

Overall:

- One-third of the marks (around 20 marks) are awarded for knowledge and understanding (AO1).
- One-third (around 20 marks) are for evaluation and comment and application to unfamiliar situations (AO2).
- One-third (around 20 marks) are for knowing about and assessing practical work, both your own and other people's.

With regard to the split over the type of questions, about 18% (around 11 marks) are involved in multiple choice questions, about 50% (around 30 marks) involve short answer questions and the remaining 32% (around 19 marks) involve extended writing, including the 12-mark essay question at the end.

In practice you can just focus on revising equal amounts of AO1, AO2 and AO3 (knowledge, evaluation and practical work) and just answer each question as it arises.

Two types of marking

There are two types of marking. One type is point-based marking, where 1 mark per point made is awarded and also there are marks for elaboration and saying more about a point. The other type of marking is called 'levels'. In this type, bands of marks are awarded according to the quality of the answer. For example, the mark scheme for a question asking for the independent variable (IV) for one of your studies for 2 marks, is:

- 0 marks — no appropriate material, e.g. giving the dependent variable (DV).
- 1 mark — not fully operationalised, such as giving one side of the IV.
- 2 marks — fully operationalised, giving both or all sides of the IV. Possibly an example is given.

Questions about your own practicals are marked according to levels and the quality. For example, if you are asked about planning your questionnaire, a thorough answer will get full marks and a weak answer will get few marks.

The essays are also marked using levels and according to quality. For example, if you are asked about two explanations for gender development and you only discuss one explanation, you will be somewhere in the middle band.

It is in the levels marking that your written skills are assessed, including how well you select material for your answer and what your spelling, grammar and use of terminology are like.

AO1, AO2 and AO3: getting it right

You must be sure to answer the question that is set — you should then cover the AO1, AO2 and/or AO3 skills.

The key words in the question (called **injunctions**, e.g. 'outline') guide what you need to write. If you answer the question, you will do what is required without worrying about the various assessment objectives.

Table 50 shows some examples of how AO1 injunctions are used and Table 51 shows examples of AO2 injunctions. Table 52 shows some examples of AO3 questions, which can include all sorts of injunctions but must be about practicals and methodology in some way.

Note that it is not so much the word itself (e.g. 'describe') that makes it AO1, AO2 or AO3, as the whole question.

The figures in brackets suggest the mark allocation you might expect for such a question.

Table 50 Examples of AO1 questions/injunctions

Type of question	What is being asked for
Describe a theory... (4)	Say what something is (a theory in this case). Imagine describing the theory to someone who knows little about the subject.
Identify a theory... (1)	Give enough information to enable the examiner to understand what is being referred to. For example, if you are asked to identify a memory theory, the answer might be 'working memory model'.
Name a theory... (1)	Name either the theory or the psychologist(s). For example, if the question asks for a memory theory, the answer might be Atkinson and Shiffrin's or the two-stage model.
Outline a definition of the...approach (2)	Follow the instructions for 'describe', but remember that this injunction requires less detail, and hence carries fewer marks.
Describe Hofling et al.'s (1966) study... (5)	Try to give the aim of the study, the method, the procedure, the results and the conclusion(s).

Table 51 Examples of AO2 questions/injunctions

Type of question	What is being asked for
Outline a strength of... (2)	You are asked to outline something, so the injunction seems to be AO1 (knowledge and understanding). However, as what is outlined is a strength (in this case) and thus you are being asked to evaluate something, this question would carry AO2 marks.
With regard to the stimulus material above, explain... (6)	You are asked to refer to some stimulus material and apply your knowledge of psychology to explain the material in some way. Refer to the material as much as possible in your answer.
Compare two theories of memory... (6)	You are asked to choose two theories of memory and then write about how they are similar and/or how they are different. And/or means you can do both or one or the other.
Assess how far cue-dependent forgetting is a useful theory... (4)	You are asked to consider practical uses of the theory of forgetting or you can evaluate the theory itself, because that would shed light on how useful it might be — but focus on its usefulness.

Table 52 Examples of AO3 questions/injunctions

Type of question	What is being asked for
Outline the aim(s) of your experiment... (2)	You are asked to say what the purpose of your study was, which is to say briefly what you were trying to find out. 'Outline' sounds like an AO1 injunction, but as this is about your practical, it is an AO3 question.
Evaluate one of these studies — either Reicher and Haslam (2006), Tafjel et al. (1970) or Sherif et al. (1954) the Robber's Cave study... (5)	You will have covered one of these studies but not all of them. Choose the one you know and give comments, criticisms, good points and so on about it. Consider the strengths and weaknesses of the research method, perhaps, or criticisms of the ethics involved. Look at alternative findings or consider whether justified conclusions are drawn. This can be an AO3 question, even though 'evaluate' sounds like an AO2 injunction. It is about someone else's study, which is psychology in practice, so it can be an AO3 question. Reicher and Haslam is explained in this guide.

Conclusions: use of injunctions and the AO1/AO2/AO3 split

Don't just think of a word in the question as being the whole question. For example, you would think 'describe' is an AO1 command because it seems to ask for knowledge, but 'describe a strength' is an AO2 injunction because it asks for evaluation, and 'describe the procedure of your practical' is an AO3 question because it asks about psychology in practice.

'Discuss' could signal AO2 marks if you are asked to 'discuss the usefulness of...'. Because you are considering how useful something is, you are doing more than showing knowledge about it. The best approach is to *answer the question*. If you study the question and understand the question, all should be well.

Sample questions

- Questions are presented in two sections, one for each of the two approaches. The separate sections will help you to revise and practise questions.
- Remember: the paper will not split the questions up by approach, so expect either of the approaches for any question. The paper will ask about any of the six areas within each approach at any time.
- Choose one approach and revise the material using this unit guide. Work through the questions for your chosen approach, answering them yourself without reading the advice on how to answer the question and without reading the answer given.
- Then mark your own answers and read through the advice on what is required. Did you interpret the question successfully? Read through the answers given and note where the marks are awarded. Finally, read through the examiner's comments to see what a full answer should include.
- Once you have prepared answers for all the questions in a particular approach, answer them again but this time choose a different topic. For example, if you answered a question on one study in detail, answer it again using the other study in detail that you have prepared. If you have described a theory of memory within the cognitive approach, describe your other chosen theory of memory. In this way you are making up your own questions, which is useful preparation for the examination.
- There are papers that you can work through, with a mark scheme and examiner's report for each paper and sample assessment materials prepared for your course. You can find materials on the Edexcel website (www.edexcel.com), so work through them as well.

Examiner's comments

All questions and answers are followed by examiner's comments. These are preceded by the icon ⓔ. They indicate where credit is due and point out areas for improvement, specific problems and common errors such as poor time management, lack of clarity, weak or non-existent development, irrelevance, misinterpretation of the question and mistaken meanings of terms. Note that there are also ticks in the answers to show where exactly marks are awarded.

Section 1 **The social approach**

Definitions

(I) In the boxes below, tick the two statements that apply to the social approach. (2 marks, AO1)

   (a) Individuals cannot be understood outside their culture ☐

   (b) Interactions between people are important ☐

   **(c) Information is processed by the brain; there is input,
      processing and output** ☐

   (d) An individual is governed most by their biological structure ☐

ⓔ This is a multiple-choice question with two right answers. Read all the statements carefully. First, identify those you think are right, and second, quickly check that the other two statements are definitely wrong. Then you can be sure you are ticking the right boxes.

Student answer

(a) Individuals cannot be understood outside their culture ☑ ✓

(b) Interactions between people are important ☑ ✓

(c) Information is processed by the brain; there is input,
    processing and output ☐

(d) An individual is governed most by their biological structure ☐

ⓔ Information processing refers to cognitive processing, and the social approach does not look at biological factors, so only the first two can be right.

(2) Describe what is meant by social psychology. (4 marks, AO1)

ⓔ This question is more likely to ask what is meant by the social approach, but get used to seeing the question asked in different ways. This is about the definition of the approach. Think about any assumptions underlying the approach. It would be useful to give an example to show understanding, but the example must be fully explained, not just mentioned.

Student answer

Social psychology looks at people as groups and how they behave in groups. ✓ For example, social identity theory suggests that self-esteem is to do with identifying with a group, and this means in-group favouritism and out-group hostility, which explains prejudice. ✓ Social psychology looks at people as social beings, including issues such as why some individuals obey others even when it goes against their own moral code. Social psychology focuses on an individual, but more on how an individual fits in with others within a society than on the individual themselves. ✓ There is a focus on interactions between people; issues such as crowd behaviour, helping others, prejudice and obedience are examples of topics covered. ✓

ⓔ This answer relies on examples quite a lot, but that is fine because they are clearly explained to show underlying principles of the approach, such as the focus on groups and interactions between individuals. If you are using an example, make sure you either give quite a few instances, as in the last point, or you explain fully, as in the second point.

(3) Explain what is meant by agentic state and in-group behaviour. In your answer give an example of each. (6 marks, AO1)

ⓔ Assume there are 3 marks for each term, and that in each case 1 of those marks is for the example. The other 2 marks in each case will be given for a clear definition, and a weaker definition will get 1 mark.

Student answer

The agentic state is a term used in Milgram's agency theory and applies to when people obey someone in authority because they give that person the power to make decisions for them ✓ and they are acting as an agent for the authority figure. ✓ An example is when soldiers act under orders rather than because of their own decision-making, or when Milgram's participants obeyed an order which they thought meant they were giving another person electric shocks. ✓ In-group behaviour refers to when people who are part of a group act according to group norms and rules that have been drawn up by the group members. ✓ They might wear a uniform or similar clothing or something that identifies them as part of a group. ✓ An example of in-group behaviour is when supporters of one football team wear the colours of the team and sing chants that they have developed. ✓

ⓔ Full marks are given here because the basic definition is there in each case, with some elaboration for the second mark. There are clear examples as well, with two examples for the explanation of 'agentic state'.

Methodology

(1) Give *one* strength and *one* weakness of surveys as a research method. (4 marks, AO3)

ⓔ There are 2 marks for the strength and 2 marks for the weakness. Do not just give a brief answer for each — be sure to expand your answer enough for the full 2 marks. For example, say what the strength is, and then say something else to explain it further or give an example.

Student answer

One strength is that a lot of people can be reached relatively cheaply by posting surveys or by handing them out in busy areas. Compared with an experiment, many participants can be reached and potentially can contribute data. ✓ ✓ A weakness is that there can be a poor response rate. When a lot of people are asked, it is likely that many will not post the questionnaire back, or that people will refuse to complete it if asked personally. A poor response rate can mean a biased sample and bias in replies. ✓ ✓

(e) A strength and a weakness are correctly identified, for 1 mark each, and there is some expansion in each case, so full marks.

> **(2) An interview using a set list of questions was carried out with 20 people who happened to be in a town on a Tuesday afternoon and agreed to take part. The aim was to find out whether people preferred those who were like them or were happier meeting and finding out about people who were different.**
>
> **(a) What type of interview was being used?**   (1 mark, AO3)

(e) You have studied three types of interview and you need to choose the one that fits this stimulus material.

Student answer

Structured interview. ✓

(e) This is the right answer — there is a set list of questions.

> **(b) What sampling was used? Explain your answer.**   (2 marks, AO3)

(e) You have studied four sampling types, and two of these will fit the stimulus material, so choose one and briefly explain this choice for the second mark.

Student answer 1

This is volunteer sampling. ✓ Only those who stopped and agreed would have completed the interview, and this would mean the participants had volunteered and were self-selecting. ✓

(e) This is right and the justification is clear, so both marks are given.

Student answer 2

Opportunity sampling. ✓

(e) This is a right answer but it needs explaining — that only those in that town on a Tuesday afternoon are going to be in the sample. There could be 1 mark for saying 'opportunity', but it is also possible that this mark will only be given if it is clear that this knowledge is accompanied by understanding (you need to show you know what opportunity sampling is). Try to do more than just name the sampling method. For this answer, 1 mark is given.

> **(c) Give two possible problems with the sampling method used.**   (2 marks, AO3)

(e) There is 1 mark for each problem, and 'give' does not mean you have to say anything about the problems. However, the problems need to be clear enough to be understood. The problems can be general issues concerning the sampling method, as the question does not say you have to relate to the stimulus material.

Student answer

Volunteer sampling means only those willing to take part do so; in this case, those with time will be in the sample, which means there is bias. ✓ Another related problem is that volunteers might be those of a certain gender, perhaps the same gender as the person carrying out the interviews, which again might mean bias. ✓

ⓔ There are 2 marks here, 1 for the factor of 'having time' and the other for 'gender'. The possible problems are clearly given.

(d) Explain two advantages of using the type of interview used. (4 marks, AO3)

ⓔ There are 2 marks for each advantage and nothing for disadvantages. To 'explain' the advantage you need to be clear about why it is good and how it relates to the type of interview, which in this case is structured interviewing.

Student answer

One advantage is the ease of analysis, because structured interviews ask all participants the same questions and the answers, therefore, can be confidently compared. ✓ Another advantage is that anyone can carry out the interview, because the questions are clearly listed and there is no deviation from them, ✓ so interviewers do not have to be trained in how to explore issues. ✓

ⓔ Only 3 marks are gained as there is not enough elaboration on the first advantage. The second advantage explains that, because there is no deviation from the questions, anyone can carry out the interviews, and then there is elaboration saying that this reduces the need for using only trained interviewers. The explanation of the first advantage, however, while noting that having the same questions means answers can be compared, does not elaborate on how this can be done or why this is useful. An elaboration could be that there is no problem with trying to compare the answers, unlike unstructured interviews, in which questions are explored further and differently for each respondent.

(e) Explain one factor that might make the findings lack validity. (2 marks, AO3)

ⓔ The question asks about validity, which refers to how 'real-life' the results will be. Consider one feature of the structured interview that would mean the results might be artificial, and make sure you say why this would be the case, so that you get the 2 marks. The question does not ask you to consider that particular structured interview (such as the sampling or the situation), but you could do.

Student answer

The interview might lack validity because the interviewer will take the respondent through the set questions even if there is more that the respondent wants to say about the issues. ✓ This restricts the respondent's answers and means that they are limited, so it is likely that they lack validity. The answers will in some ways be forced because of the questions. ✓ In some structured interviews some questions are closed questions, which would mean even more forced-choice answers.

ⓔ This answer is thorough and gets both marks. The factor is identified as the restrictions that set questions impose, and the answer then explains this more fully by saying that this means the answer cannot be expanded beyond the question, which in turn means that 'real' answers might not be given. You can see that even though there are only 2 marks, the answer has to be reasonably thorough to make sure the points are clear.

> **(f) Given what you know about social identity, what would you expect to find from the interview? Explain your answer.**   (2 marks, AO3)

ⓔ You do not have to explain social identity theory here, but you could summarise it briefly and then link to the aim of the interview and what results would be expected.

Student answer 1

You would expect that people prefer their own in-group. ✓

ⓔ This is limited but is a brief statement of what would be expected and is accurate, so is likely to get 1 mark.

Student answer 2

Social identity theory suggests that self-esteem comes from being in a group with others and identifying with that group — which is then treated as better than an out-group so that self-esteem is good. So it would be expected that people prefer people from their in-group, operationalised as being 'like them', rather than people from the out-group, operationalised as people who are 'different'. ✓ ✓

ⓔ This answer gets both marks because the link to social identity theory is clear and the question is answered clearly too — people are more likely to like people in their in-group than those in their out-group.

Content

> **(1) What is meant by the term 'obedience'?**   (2 marks, AO1)

ⓔ You need to give a definition of obedience. A simple definition will gain 1 mark and a more detailed definition will gain the 2 marks.

Student answer

Obedience is when people obey others in authority. ✓

ⓔ This gets 1 mark because it is right but not worth both marks. It is not enough to say that obedience is when people obey, but saying that they obey others in authority is enough for 1 mark. For full marks, this needs more detail, such as mentioning that obeying means you are in an agentic state, or saying that it differs from conformity in that someone is acting upon orders and might not agree. More needs to be said, such as 'following orders' rather than 'obey', because 'obey' is obvious. It is good to give an example, such as when someone moves a car because a parking attendant tells them to.

(2) Describe Milgram's agency theory of obedience. (4 marks, AO1)

ⓔ There are 4 marks here, all for describing what is meant by the agency theory. An example is a good idea, but keep it short as it is worth no more than 1 mark. However, it helps to illustrate your answer and show that you understand the theory.

Student answer

In Milgram's study, the participants denied to themselves that they were responsible for their actions. They allowed the experimenter to take responsibility for what was happening. When you are not acting under your own control but because of the orders of someone else, you are their agent, and this is called being in an agentic state. ✓ ✓

ⓔ 2 marks are awarded here for saying what an agentic state is, although the answer is not well focused on the question. The other 2 marks could be gained by linking this to Milgram's study and showing that the participants said they felt they had to continue and were just obeying orders. This was his agency theory of obedience — that people were not making their own decisions. The answer could have said that the opposite of the agentic state is being autonomous and acting on one's own decisions, whereas being in an agentic state means doing what someone in authority says, which is probably necessary in order for society to function. This could possibly be due to someone being brought up in that way, or possibly because of inherited tendencies.

(3) Evaluate social identity theory as an explanation of prejudice. (4 marks, AO2)

ⓔ Note that for 'evaluate' questions you do not have to describe at all. Assume that the examiner knows what the theory is. All 4 marks are for evaluation. You could say that another theory explains prejudice better or contradicts this one, or you could criticise the research methods used to arrive at the theory (perhaps researchers used laboratory experiments that are not valid). If you mention an alternative theory there is likely to be only 1 mark, because if you then start looking more at that alternative theory you are addressing a different question.

Student answer

Many studies have shown that we prefer our in-group and are less interested in any out-group, and their findings are evidence for the theory. Tajfel did a lot of work in this area, and others have too. It seems that we boost our self-esteem by siding with an in-group, which means going against an out-group. So social identity theory (SIT) seems a reasonable explanation and we have evidence for it. ✓ It can also explain the findings of other studies of prejudice, even if they are said to be about another theory. For example, Minard carried out a study of miners. The study could be explained by saying that the miners were an in-group when working, but when above ground, they were no longer an in-group (not being 'miners' any more but going home to different roles). ✓ Also Sherif's study at Robbers Cave, although arriving at the theory of realistic conflict as an explanation of prejudice, did look at in-group and out-group behaviour between the Rattlers and Eagles and found out-group hostility, as social identity theory predicts. ✓ However, much of the research was done using experiments and falsely formed groups, so the conclusions might not be valid. ✓

(e) Full marks are gained here. 1 mark is awarded for saying that there is a lot of evidence (although this needs elaboration, as is done here, by giving Tajfel). A further mark is given for the Minard example and showing how SIT can explain it. Minard is probably a new study for you and shows that it is useful to go beyond your textbook. But you could add more about evidence (e.g. experiments are reliable) to get the final mark. Another mark is for the reference to the theory being useful in explaining Sherif's findings. The final mark is for the methodological criticism of the lack of validity.

Studies in detail

(1) Describe Hofling et al. (1966) — a study from the social approach.   (5 marks, AO1)

(e) Note that just describing what was done in the study (the procedure), or what was found (the results or findings), is not enough for all 5 marks. One way of getting the marks is to assume that up to 2 marks can be gained for saying why the study was done, which is the aim. Up to 2 more marks can be gained by saying what was done, which is the procedure. There are up to 2 marks for saying what was found (the results). A maximum of 2 marks can also be earned for giving the conclusions. There are more ways than one to get the 5 marks. These ideas apply if the question asks for the whole study to be described. There could, however, be a question about one of the elements (e.g. procedure, results) that asks for more than 2 marks, so you need to prepare more, as is advised in the content section of this book.

Student answer

Hofling studied a group of 22 nurses in the main field experiment. The nurses were on duty and were given instructions over the phone by a doctor who wanted them to give a patient a dosage of a drug — however, this dosage would have been too high. ✓ Although the nurses should not have taken instructions over the phone, and they should have checked the dosage, 21 out of the 22 nurses obeyed the doctor. ✓ They were stopped before the drug was administered, and there was no real medication in any case. ✓ The study was to find out whether nurses would obey orders when they knew they should not. ✓

(e) The first mark is for the procedure, although a little more detail would have earned 2 marks. The main result (21 out of 22 obeyed) is given, and gets 1 mark. A mark is awarded for the information that they were stopped and in any case there was no real drug, as this is elaboration upon the procedure. A further mark could have been gained by drawing a clear conclusion about obedience to authority. The aim is given at the end and gets a mark too. So 4 marks are awarded out of 5. More could have been said about the findings, and 'findings' means results and/or conclusions. Note with 2 procedure marks having been given, there are no more available given the likelihood of there being a maximum of 2 marks for this element of the study.

(2) Evaluate Hofling et al. (1966) — a study from the social approach.   (5 marks, AO2)

(e) Evaluation of studies can come in many forms. You can give ethical issues (good and/or bad), alternative theories or studies, methodological problems (such as the reliability of experiments or the limitations of case studies) or criticisms of the study itself. Be sure to write enough for 5 marks. You are trying to say five things, although it is possible to gain more than 1 mark for a good, well made point. This question could be AO3, because the methodology and study findings are going to be evaluated, but if the answer includes evaluation using another study or a theory, such as saying that the study reinforces Milgram's agency theory, it could be argued that that is AO2.

Student answer

The nurses were carrying out instructions in response to the doctor's authority. As part of the study, nurses in a control group were asked if they would obey instructions such as those given in the study, and they all said they would not. This shows that the situation we are in and the social pressure at the time influences our behaviour, which is a useful contribution. ✓ As this study was a field study and took place in a real hospital with real nurses, it was thought to be stronger evidence of obedience than Milgram's artificial laboratory study. The study has ecological validity (validity with regard to setting and situation). ✓ ✓ Nurses were taken from different hospitals, so possibly generalisation is okay, but all the nurses were female, so there may have been an issue in generalising to male nurses. The obedience could have been because the 'doctor' was male and the nurse female. ✓ ✓

ⓔ 1 mark is achieved for pointing out the usefulness of the contribution, and 2 marks for comparing the study with Milgram's and showing that Hofling's study is arguably more valid. This is a double mark because there is quite a bit of information, and if you gave just some of it you would get 1 mark. A further double mark is given because the issue of generalisation is given in some detail, with examples as to why it might be a problem. So this answer gets all 5 marks.

(3) Describe the findings (results and/or conclusions) of either Reicher and Haslam (2003/2006), the Sherif et al. (1954) Robbers Cave study or Tajfel et al. (1970/1971) — studies from the social approach.
(5 marks, AO1)

ⓔ The results and/or conclusions (findings) of one of the listed studies are asked for. 5 marks are quite a lot, so details are needed. It would be wise to give both the results and the conclusions. Focus on results and/or conclusions and do not describe what happened in the study. Do make sure it is identifiable, but it should be if the results and/or conclusions are accurate. In this book Reicher and Haslam (2003/2006) has been explained, but the other studies are included here for your interest or in case you covered one of them in your course instead of Reicher and Haslam.

Student answer 1

Reicher and Haslam found that participants who were given the role of prisoner formed an in-group and worked as a group as well as identifying with the group. ✓ However, the guards did not form into a group and did not work as a team. ✓ There were five guards, and it was noticed that the strongest personalities were among the prisoners, which may have led to the strength of the prisoners. ✓ As the prisoners grew stronger as a group, they overcame the authority of the guards and a commune-style system was developed by agreement of all the participants. ✓ However, this did not last, and by the end of the study the participants had agreed that they needed a strong system to achieve the aims they had been set. ✓

ⓔ This answer works through the results and is clear and detailed. No real conclusions are given, except perhaps the fact that the strongest personalities being found among the prisoners might have led to the results — though that in itself is like a result. Each point gets a mark, as it is clearly expressed. More about the conclusions would have added marks if they were needed. For example, they found that social identity theory was supported by the findings of the study and identification with an in-group helped with decision-making and forming group norms.

Student answer 2

Sherif et al. found that the boys formed two in-groups and quickly formed leader–follower relations as well as setting up group norms so that decisions could be made. ✓ Once each in-group knew about the other, they were quickly hostile towards the out-group and started to call them names, for example. ✓ They wanted to compete with the out-group. Competition led to hostility and friction. ✓ Finally, working towards superordinate goals reduced the friction, but only after they had to work together for quite a few such goals (e.g. reinstating the water supply). ✓ ✓

ⓔ This answer also gets the full 5 marks because of the detail given. The last point about superordinate goals gets a double mark because it mentions that more than one superordinate goal had to be worked towards for reduction of prejudice, which is an elaboration of the point about working towards superordinate goals. Also, the use of the term enriches that part of the answer.

Student answer 3

Tajfel et al. set up minimal groups by falsely suggesting that individuals liked either Klee or Kandinsky and that that put them into a special group. He set up a study where the participants had to give rewards either to their own group members or to individuals from the other group, the out-group. It was found that even when minimal groups were formed, the members of the in-group still favoured their own members against out-group members. ✓

ⓔ This only gets 1 mark because a lot more detail is needed about the results and/or conclusions. The answer is spoiled because a lot of it focuses on the procedure of the study, which is not asked for, so that bit gets no marks. This shows the importance of answering the question.

Key issue

(1) Read the source below. Then explain what is being said, using concepts from the social approach.

(6 marks, AO2)

Fighting broke out between two local villages when a visiting rugby team from one of the villages won an annual competition by 28 points. At first, the fight was only between two of the players who had clashed during the match, but soon the fighting spread and police had to be called. Elders from one of the villages explained that there had been prejudice between the two villages for years, ever since a factory was built near one village. This had brought good road links and jobs, whereas the other village was in another valley and did not have the same advantages.

(e) This extract is clearly focusing on groups, which suggests that social identity theory is a good one to choose in order to explain the extract. If you have studied the Sherif study, you could also look at the idea that competition leads to hostility between groups and working towards superordinate goals can help to reduce the hostility. If you have studied Tajfel's study about minimal groups, you can use the findings to help to explain the extract. The Reicher and Haslam study also looks at the success of an in-group structure, so can be used. When studying the social approach you will have looked at what the approach is about in general, such as how behaviour has to be understood in terms of groups and cultures, and those concepts can also be useful for this answer. Remember to refer to the source at least once in your answer to show you are clearly focusing on the question.

Student answer

Social identity theory claims that prejudice arises when an in-group becomes hostile to an out-group, possibly to enhance the self-esteem of the in-group. ✓ In the source passage, the villagers in each case would probably form an in-group, including not only those who were team members but the whole village. ✓ This would be more likely if one village were seen to be better off than the other, as was the case here. This is an example of scapegoating — where people are blamed for problems they are not responsible for, and prejudice forms. ✓ Prejudice can lead to aggression through frustration, and economic disadvantages can lead to frustration. ✓

(e) Two concepts of how prejudice might occur (SIT and scapegoating) are given here, and each earns marks. In each case, 1 mark is for giving the concept accurately, and for SIT, 1 mark is for linking well to the passage. A fourth mark is given for suggesting that frustration might cause the aggression. This links to the frustration–aggression hypothesis, which you may not have studied, but is a good, relevant point from social psychology and shows that you can bring in material from anywhere within the approach. Further marks could have been scored by adding that in this case, the villages were in competition, but if another situation arose where they had to work together (to solve a superordinate goal, for example), prejudice might be reduced, which links to Sherif's study. Ideas from crowd behaviour could also have been used successfully here, as well as evidence from the other studies that are suggested for the 'Studies in detail' section of the course. If you stick to what you have learned in the course, that is fine — and you could have gone into more depth about social categorisation, social comparison and social identity, using the theory to get more marks.

(2) Social psychology can be used to help us understand key issues in psychology. Describe *one* such key issue.

(4 marks, AO1)

(e) The main point here is to describe the issue, not the psychology that helps to explain it. Avoid mentioning studies, theories or concepts as far as you can, because they are the explanations of the issue, not the description. Sometimes you have to use concepts, because the issue is about such concepts — for example, if you choose prejudice. However, most concepts can be avoided — for example, refer to two groups in conflict, not to in-group and out-group, if you are talking about football hooliganism.

Student answer

In recent years there have been occasions when members of armed forces have been charged as individuals for brutal acts. ✓ One example is when US soldiers were photographed treating prisoners in the Abu Ghraib prison in Iraq in a humiliating and brutal way. ✓ Soldiers are supposed to treat prisoners of war carefully and with respect for their position, and there are rules and conventions. ✓ The pictures were published in the media and there was a general outcry from around the world against soldiers using their position of power in such a way. It was hard to understand how they could do this, given their training. ✓

e This answer is clear enough and marks are given quite quickly, as it is not easy to stick to describing only the issue — which is how this could happen and what would make them do it. The first mark is for the general idea that soldiers should not commit brutal acts, though this is not yet fully explained in the answer. The second mark is for the actual example. The third mark is for one side of the issue — that soldiers are not supposed to do this. The fourth mark is for the actual issue — that it is hard to understand why this would happen, with the implication that such behaviour needs to be explained.

(3) Use concepts and ideas from the social approach to explain one key issue that you have studied. In your answer make the key issue clear.   (6 marks, AO1)

e This question is asking you to choose a key issue and apply what you know about social psychology to help to explain the issue. The marks are AO1 marks because you will be describing what you have learned rather than applying it to a novel situation, as is done in question 1 in this section. Use terminology as much as you can, to give a good answer. You can use studies to help to explain the concepts. Here answers are given on two issues other than the Abu Ghraib situation that was chosen as the key issue for this book. This is because it is useful for you to know about other issues, in order to prepare for an issue you might be presented with in the examination. You do not have to know these other issues or explanations, but it is useful to know a little bit more about the approach for this section.

Student answer 1

A key issue that can be explained using ideas from the social approach is football hooliganism. One concept is deindividuation. People do things when they are anonymous that they would not otherwise do. ✓ They get carried away by the behaviour of the crowd around them, and follow the actions of another person. This idea of being carried away has been called social contagion. ✓ Ethnocentricity is another concept. This is the rejection of the out-group and the focus on the in-group. ✓ In a football crowd, the in-group would be the supporters of the team the individual supports, and the out-group would be supporters of the other team. ✓ So whatever the in-group is doing, that person would follow, and this would lead to prejudice towards the out-group — and possibly violence. ✓ Social identity theory explains that people identify with their in-group and think positively about its members, whereas they think negatively about the out-group members. This helps to increase their self-esteem. ✓ Football supporters are out-groups if they support the 'other' team, so there would be hostility towards the out-group.

(e) This answer gets all the marks. The first mark is for the idea of deindividuation, which is summarised to show it is understood. The second mark is for social contagion, another theory of crowd behaviour. You may not have come across these two concepts, because you have not prepared this key issue — and in fact you can discuss football hooliganism without mentioning these concepts. Just use the concepts you know and have prepared. A third mark is given for the link to in-groups and out-groups, and another mark for the elaboration of this point by showing how the idea of in-group and out-group fits with football supporters. The fifth mark is good because there is a link to violence, which is what hooliganism is about. And the final mark is for elaborating on the idea of social identity theory and mentioning the link with self-esteem.

Student answer 2

Control of crowd behaviour is something that has been investigated in the social approach. In particular, in this country (and others) football crowds have become violent, and this has spoilt enjoyment for many and cost a lot in terms of policing (and injuries). The social approach has shown that people are deindividuated in a crowd and may do things they would not otherwise do. ✓ If video cameras are used, or if only season ticket-holders are allowed into the game, this might prevent deindividuation, because individuals could be identified. ✓ This should help to prevent football hooliganism. Crowds can also be affected by emotional contagion, where emotions spread to those around, and previously calm individuals may become violent. ✓ A way of avoiding this is to keep the crowd calm. If people do not all stand together but stadiums are all-seating with no standing, this might help to avoid pressure. It could be that reactions come from biological stresses, which means social psychology is not the only explanation. ✓ Social psychology studies can be experimental, which means the situation can be unnatural and so not applicable to real life. However, many studies are done in the field as observations, and much can be discovered from these because they are studying real crowd situations and real crowd behaviour, so there is validity. ✓

(e) This is a good answer up to a point, and at the end it starts to consider evaluation. There are some good points, such as biological factors being important, and also the fact that many studies are not done in natural situations so there is no validity, which means findings are in doubt and 2 marks are given for this evaluation. Deindividuation gets a mark, and another mark is given for elaboration, as the answer suggests how to avoid the problem. A mark is given for social contagion too, so 5 marks are given in all. Other marks could be achieved by talking about realistic conflict if the crowd has formed because of some pressure or problem. The idea of superordinate goals could be discussed in that case, helping to show how to reduce pressure. Football crowds are mentioned, so the idea of in-group and out-group could be used, as in the previous answer.

Practical

For the social approach, you will have carried out either a questionnaire or an interview. Answer the following questions with your practical in mind.

(1) (a) What is the aim of the practical?   (2 marks, AO3)

e Expect to give the aim of each of your practicals — the aim usually has 2 marks. Just be clear, giving the research method if appropriate and what you were trying to find out — this often includes a brief mention of the IV and the DV, but this might not be appropriate. You do not need to give full detail of these variables.

Student answer

My questionnaire was to find out, using both open and closed questions, if people think those in their in-group are better than others who are in the out-group. This is to test the social identity theory. ✓ ✓

e This is fine, as it gives the research method, the types of questions and the independent variable as well as the overall aim of testing the theory. Well worth the 2 marks.

(b) Give two examples of what was asked/what was in the interview schedule.   (2 marks, AO3)

e You need to give two questions here — either questionnaire or interview questions. Here it is assumed that the practical was a questionnaire to look at social identity theory. You don't need to be exact about what you actually asked, just make sure the questions are appropriate to your aim.

Student answer

Do you like people in your group better than those in other groups? Yes No ✓

When you are with people you don't know very well, does that make you feel less confident? Yes No ✓

e These two questions are fine and would work. You might think of problems with them, but the idea is just to test the sort of questions that could be asked and they don't have to be perfect.

(c) Why did you include personal data?   (2 marks, AO3)

e Personal data are data about the individual rather than about the IV. The question asks you to talk about why that is needed, rather than which personal data you asked for. You could answer by referring to the actual personal data you gathered — but remember to say why.

Student answer

Personal data are needed to check the data against. For example, I asked about gender because I wanted to know if there is a gender difference in in-group preferences. ✓

e This gets 1 mark because the example makes the first sentence clear, but on its own the first sentence is not particularly helpful. The answer needed to say what 'check against' means. Another example might have got you another mark, if the example was detailed enough. Or the answer could say more about what personal data are.

(d) Explain one ethical decision you made. (2 marks, AO3)

ⓔ Choose one ethical issue you considered — even if you did not address it well. Then explain the issue and what you did about it (or why you did not).

Student answer

I was careful to get informed consent. I put standardised instructions on the top of my questionnaire and said it was about in-group and out-group behaviour and that the findings would only be used for my course. I said that no names were required and that data were confidential. This told the respondent about the study, so they were informed. Then I just asked them if it was okay to continue, which meant consent was given and informed. ✓ ✓

ⓔ This is a thorough answer and gets the 2 marks.

(e) Choose whether a survey is a reliable or a valid research method and explain your answer. (2 marks, AO3)

ⓔ Choose to look at either reliability or validity and then, having chosen, discuss your research method with that issue in mind. Note that this question asks about a survey in general, not about your *own* survey.

Student answer

A survey has good reliability because there are set questions and they are repeated for all respondents. So the answers, which often give quantitative data, can be compared. ✓ Questions should be clear, following a pilot study, so that if they were asked again the same responses would be found. ✓

ⓔ There is enough here for the 2 marks. This answer clearly shows understanding of what reliability is and mentions the issues of closed questions, comparability and a pilot study, all of which are useful issues with regard to reliability.

Section 2 **The cognitive approach**

Definitions

(1) Outline one factor that a definition of the cognitive approach might include.   (3 marks, AO1)

ⓔ This question asks for an outline, which is a brief description. One way of getting 1 mark is to give an example, but you would need to outline the factor first. Think of something about the approach and write it down. Then explain it a bit more to elaborate. Then think of an example of this factor within the approach.

Student answer

The mind/brain processes information. ✓ We take information in, and then it is subjected to mental processes. There is input, processing and then output.✓ For example, we take information in via the senses, process it according to the multi-store model of memory, through two stores — the short-term store and the long-term store — and then there is an output if we remember the information. ✓

ⓔ This is a clear and concise answer. 1 mark is given for the factor, in this case that we process information. 1 mark is awarded for linking this to the processing of information and for expanding on this by mentioning input, processing and output. There could have been 2 marks here if the idea of mental processes had been expanded as well. The example of the multi-store model gained the final mark as it is clear and used effectively. Note that just saying that the multi-store model is an example is not enough — you have to show how it is an example.

(2) Tick two of the following statements that are features of the cognitive approach.   (2 marks, AO1)

    (a) **According to the cognitive approach we are guided strongly by our unconscious** ☐

    (b) **The approach holds that there are similarities in the ways computers and brains operate** ☐

    (c) **The approach holds that information is processed by the brain; there is input, processing and output** ☐

    (d) **The approach focuses on why we behave as we do in groups** ☐

ⓔ This is straightforward in that there are two correct statements and two are not about the cognitive approach. This would be a multiple-choice question and you would put ticks in the boxes provided.

Student answer

(a) According to the cognitive approach we are guided strongly by our unconscious ☐

(b) The approach holds that there are similarities in the ways computers and brains operate ☑✓

(c) The approach holds that information is processed by the brain; there is input, processing and output ☑✓

(d) The approach focuses on why we behave as we do in groups ☐

ⓔ These choices are correct, for 2 marks.

(3) Using information from cognitive psychology, explain what is meant by saying that the information processing approach could include input, processing and output. (3 marks, AO1)

ⓔ You would expect to be asked about the cognitive approach in general, but prepare for questions like this to help with detail. You can use one of the memory theories you studied or one of the forgetting theories — or any other ideas and concepts you know about.

Student answer 1

The levels of processing approach suggests that what is input, such as the type of question, leads to different processing ✓ and different output, such as whether the 'yes' or 'no' response is activated and how this affects whether a word is recognised or not. ✓ For example, if a question asks whether one word rhymes with another word, the words are input ✓ and the processing involves whether the words rhyme or not. ✓ This is likely to include referring to previously stored information in some way. Following the processing a 'yes' or 'no' response occurs, which is the output. ✓

ⓔ This answer is given five ticks, although there is some repetition in the answer. The ticks are given to show where marks are possible.

Student answer 2

The interference theory of forgetting shows how information is input, processing occurs and then this processing affects the output. The multi-store model suggests that there is short-term and long-term memory and that interference in long-term memory depends on what has been stored previously. ✓ Information is input through the senses — sight, sound, taste and so on ✓ — and then processing takes place. Processing is through the short-term and then, for storage to take place more permanently, the long-term memory (LTM). ✓ Then there is output, depending on what is to be recalled, but output can be affected by interference at the processing stage. ✓ This means there is forgetting.

ⓔ This answer also gets full marks (there are four ticks just to show where marks might be given). The theory is clearly linked to input, processing and output.

Methodology

(1) Outline *one* strength *and* one weakness of the experiment as a research method.   (4 marks, AO3)

ⓔ There are 2 marks for the strength and 2 marks for the weakness. Don't just give a brief answer for each: be sure to expand it enough for the full 2 marks. For example, say what the strength is and then expand on what you mean.

Student answer

A strength is that it is well controlled. A weakness is that you cannot see natural behaviour, as the experiment is in a laboratory. ✓

ⓔ The weakness gets 1 mark because the answer clearly and effectively communicates that natural behaviour is not found in a laboratory. For the additional mark, this needs elaborating, perhaps mentioning the lack of validity, or saying that the unnatural situation means that what is being measured is not 'normal'. The strength does not earn a mark. The answer needs to say *what* is well controlled, and how that means that a study can be repeated to see if the same results are found, which means it has reliability, or at least something about why good controls are a strength.

(2) Name three types of experiment.   (1 mark, AO3)

ⓔ There might be more marks for a question like this, but it is more likely that there would be just 1 mark as the question only asks for a list.

Student answer

Field, laboratory and natural. ✓

ⓔ This is fine, and the question does not need any more, but it is always a good idea to spell everything out, so adding 'experiment' here would make the answer complete.

(3) Here are some data from a study.

Table 1 Number of words recognised from a list of 30, according to whether the words were processed structurally, phonemically or semantically (repeated measures design)

Participant	Structurally processed (Is the word in capitals?)	Phonemically processed (Does the word rhyme with...?)	Semantically processed (Does the word fit in this sentence?)
1	3	7	21
2	4	9	18
3	2	10	24
4	8	12	16
5	5	14	20

Participant	Structurally processed (Is the word in capitals?)	Phonemically processed (Does the word rhyme with...?)	Semantically processed (Does the word fit in this sentence?)
6	7	8	17
7	10	12	16
8	4	16	18
9	3	8	12
10	4	8	24
Mean	5	10.4	18.6
Median	4	9.5	18
Mode	4	8	16/18/24
Range	8	9	12

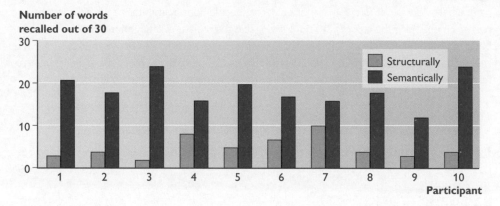

Number of words recalled out of 30

Figure 1 Number of words recalled, whether processed structurally or semantically

(3) (a) Which type of processing led to more words being recalled on average? Explain your answer.

(2 marks, AO3)

ⓔ You need to choose one or more of the averages (mean, median or mode, though when the word 'average' is used it usually refers to the mean, so that would be a suitable choice) and give the figures to explain your answer.

Student answer

The mean average shows that the semantic processing gave the most recall, the phonemic the next best recall and structural processing the worst recall. ✓ The worst recall gave a mean average of 5.0 words of the 30 (structural), the next best gave a mean average of 10.4 (phonemic) and the best recall gave a mean average of 18.6 words out of 30. ✓ The median and the mode showed the same pattern. ✓

ⓔ This answer is thorough and gives the answer in figures as well as words, which strengthens it. Where possible, include figures in such an answer. There are three ticks, though only 2 marks are available.

(b) Summarise what the graph shows.

(2 marks, AO3)

ⓔ You need to show the trends the graph illustrates. Say enough for the 2 marks, so more than just one brief sentence.

Student answer

The graph shows that every participant recalls more words when asked if a word fits into a sentence (semantic processing) than if asked whether a word is in capital letters (structural processing). ✓ In all but one case, twice as many (or more) words are recalled when using semantic processing, which shows the size of the difference. ✓

ⓔ The first sentence is the main answer, but you need more for the second mark — looking at the size of the difference is a good idea as it is a clear feature of this graph.

(c) Explain how to find the median and the mode of a set of numbers.

(4 marks, AO3)

ⓔ If you needed to, you could work out how the two measures of central tendency are calculated, because the table shows this. There are 2 marks for each explanation, so you could use an example to illustrate for the second mark.

Student answer

The median is the middle score of a set of scores, ✓ and if there is an even number of scores (such as 10, as here), the median is in the middle of the scores and has to be calculated (such as midway between scores 5 and 6 here). ✓ If there is an odd number of scores (such as 11), the median is in the middle and it is easier to find, as it will be the score at position 6. The mode is the score found most often, ✓ and to calculate it means looking to see which score appears the most times. ✓ If there is not just one score in this position, but more, all those scores appear against the mode — there is no single mode. This is the case for the semantic processing condition in this example.

ⓔ There is more here than is needed for the 4 marks, because the first mark is given for a basic definition of the two terms and then another mark is given for elaboration. Don't assume that this quick early mark is being awarded, and give more explanation, as is done here. It is always better to show understanding of the issue(s) in as much depth as possible — bearing in mind time restraints, of course.

Content

(1) Outline *one* theory of forgetting.

(3 marks, AO1)

ⓔ Giving one theory of forgetting earns you the first mark. Then there are 2 more marks for expanding on your answer. Say what the theory is, and make sure you say enough about it for the 2 extra marks.

Student answer

Retrieval failure — the cues for recall ✓ do not match the encoding that takes place in memory. ✓

ⓔ Retrieval failure due to lack of cues scores 1 mark for the theory, and the additional information about cues not matching encoding gets another 1 mark. However, this is not a clear outline of a theory of forgetting. You would need to be clearer, to talk about cue-dependent forgetting and to mention state and context dependency. This answer scores 2 marks out of 3, but only just.

(2) Evaluate *one* theory or model of memory in terms of *two* of the following criteria: methodological issues, ethical issues, alternative theories, research evidence for contradictory claims or its practical application. **(6 marks, AO2)**

ⓔ You have to do two things here and there are 6 marks. There could be up to 4 marks for each criterion used. Choose one of the criteria (e.g. ethical issues) and say three or four things about ethical issues in relation to your chosen theory of memory. Then choose one of the other criteria (e.g. alternative theories) and say three or four things about alternative theories. You can get marks by elaborating a point, so, for example, if you choose ethics and talk about one ethical issue in depth, you could gain more than 1 mark, or you could gain marks by looking at different ethical issues.

Student answer

The multi-store model has stimulated much research into the mind to identify exactly how memory is used and stored. This stimulated research by Baddeley and Hitch, who came up with the working memory (WM) model. ✓ The WM model expands short-term memory (STM) to look at four different areas. These include an articulatory loop, a visuospatial scratchpad and a central executive. ✓ Research is based on experimental evidence, which is said to lack validity as artificial tasks are used (such as using nonsense syllables). ✓

ⓔ The first criterion covered is alternative theory, and for this 2 marks are gained. 1 mark is for the mention of the model having stimulated research such as the working memory model. The second mark is for mentioning the four areas of the working model, and elaborating on this. The second criterion is methodological issues, and a mark is given for mentioning the artificial nature of experiments used. This could have been explained more fully, for the final 2 marks. For example, it could be said that learning lists underwater, as was done in Godden and Baddeley's study, is not a normal thing to do.

(3) For *one* model/theory of memory that you have studied, complete the following table. **(3 marks, AO1)**

Instruction regarding the model or theory	Answer
Identify the model/theory	
State one aspect of the model/theory	
State one problem with the model/theory	

Ⓔ There is 1 mark for each element. The first mark is for naming the model (or identifying it if you cannot recall the name of the theory or the name(s) of the researcher(s)). The second mark is for saying something about that model — for example, if looking at the multi-store model, saying that the focus is on two stores: STM and LTM. The third mark is for saying something to criticise it.

Student answer

Instruction regarding the model or theory	Answer
Identify the model/theory	Levels of processing, Craik and Lockhart (1972)
State one aspect of the model/theory	Three levels of processing are found — structural, phonemic and semantic
State one problem with the model/theory	Circular, in not really explaining anything; better recall comes from deeper processing, and we show deeper processing by pointing to better recall

Ⓔ Each of the above answers scores 1 mark. This answer gets full marks.

(4) Compare the two models/theories of forgetting that you have studied for your course. (4 marks, AO2)

Ⓔ You need to make four comparison points, clearly stating both sides of the point, to get the full marks. You could consider research methods (similarities or differences), what is being looked at (similarities or differences), the historical time when the theory/model was developed (similar or different), or any other feature you think of. Of course, both will be within cognitive psychology but that is fairly obvious, as is the fact that both are about forgetting, so it is best to avoid such answers.

Student answer

Cue-dependent forgetting is similar to interference theory because both are studied using lists of words to see under what circumstances words are forgotten. Godden and Baddeley (1975) asked divers to learn lists of words either on land or underwater and then to recall them. To test retroactive and proactive interference, different word lists are given and recalled (either the first or the second list is recalled), which is a similar procedure. ✓ ✓ Both theories use experiments to study the explanation of forgetting, and often the experiments are laboratory experiments. ✓ Cue-dependent theory considers features in the environment and how they affect remembering and forgetting, whereas interference theory looks at features in the brain to see how forgetting is affected. ✓ However, cue-dependent theory does consider how the absence of the right cues for processing causes forgetting, so both are about information processing, as would be expected in cognitive psychology. ✓

Ⓔ This answer gets the 4 marks and there are possibly 5 marks, but some of the points are not clearly made so only just get the mark. Aim for a more complete point each time. For example, saying that they both use words does not quite get the mark, though giving the two clear elaboration points afterwards means 2 marks are given together then. Saying that both use laboratory experiments is also rather weak but just gets the mark here. Include something more, e.g. they both have a clearly operationalised IV and a measurable DV. The comment about both looking at information processing but one being more concerned with internal processes is a useful one and there is some elaboration. It could, however, have been clearer, because cues are recorded from the cognitive environment in cue-dependent forgetting, which is an internal feature.

Studies in detail

(1) You will have studied Godden and Baddeley's divers study and one other from Peterson and Peterson, Craik and Tulving and Ramponi et al. Compare Godden and Baddeley's study with one of the other three in terms of the methodology used. (6 marks, AO3)

(e) When asked to compare, you need to give similarities and/or differences, and for this question you need to look at methodology. A good idea is to think of all aspects of the methodology of one of the studies and say how the other is the same or different in that aspect. Another way is to think of methodological issues and say how the two are similar or different with regard to those issues. Remember to compare and to say explicitly that one is 'XXX' (some feature), whereas the other is 'YYY' (a different feature), for example. In this guide the studies chosen are Godden and Baddeley (1975) and Craik and Tulving (1975), but the other two from the course are given here in case you studied them instead. Also knowing a bit about them will be useful, as you might be able to use the study in the key issue or in evaluation. You do not have to know another study, though, other than Godden and Baddeley and one of the other three.

Student answer 1

Both of the studies look at cognitive processes, so in that way they are similar. However, Peterson and Peterson focus more on remembering, with Godden and Baddeley looking at forgetting. They both used experiments as the research method. ✓ Godden and Baddeley used a repeated measures design and Peterson and Peterson set up two experimental procedures in their study, one of which used independent groups, so the designs were different. ✓ Godden and Baddeley used lists of words and Peterson and Peterson had lists of consonants that they used one by one, so in a way the two were similar because they both used words or letters that were recalled or not. ✓ Both studies were very carefully controlled so that only the IV was varied, and the DV could be said to be caused by the variation in the IV. ✓ For example, Godden and Baddeley tried to ensure that moving from water to land for one group did not cause disruption that would not apply to the other group, ✓ and Peterson and Peterson were careful not to use the same consonants more than once for each participant. ✓

(e) The first mark is given for saying they both use experiments, though it could have done with more detail. The detail comes later, however, when cause and effect and controls are mentioned. The second mark is for comparing the designs, and this time there is almost enough for 2 marks — 1 is given, though, because of that fairly quick first mark. The third mark is for saying their stimulus materials are similar and the fourth for mentioning good controls and elaborating a bit with comments about the IV and DV. The fifth and sixth marks are for giving the detail about the controls, one example for each study. Notice that the first two points about cognitive processes and focusing on memory or forgetting are good comparison points but get no marks, because this question was about methodology.

Student answer 2

Both Godden and Baddeley and Ramponi et al. use experiments as their research methodology, and both are trying to isolate single variables that they can test to find out about cognitive processes. ✓ Godden and Baddeley use fewer participants than Ramponi et al., because there are not many divers they can use, whereas Ramponi et al. have a large sample of both older and younger participants. ✓ Godden and Baddeley use 18 participants and altogether Ramponi et al. use 96. ✓ Both studies involve memory testing of some sort using words somehow, so in that way they are similar. ✓ Godden and Baddeley work in the field with their participants in that they are diving in any case and the study works around them, whereas Ramponi et al. set the whole study up for the purposes of gathering the data exclusively — which makes the two studies different with regard to validity. ✓ It could be said that the Godden and Baddeley study was more valid because the divers were doing what they did anyway, but they did not usually learn lists of words with special equipment, so really it was no more valid than Ramponi et al. ✓

ⓔ Again, this answer gets all 6 marks. There is a lot of detail. There are almost 2 marks in the first sentence because it says that both use experiments, as the previous answer did, and then adds a bit more. However, it was thought that the two points together were worth 1 mark rather than 2. The second mark with regard to their variables is given when the answer mentions them both using words somehow. The point about the number of participants is detailed and so gets 2 marks, and the point about validity is detailed and gets 2 marks.

Student answer 3

Both Godden and Baddeley and Craik and Tulving use experiment as their research method and use careful controls, such as with regard to the stimulus materials, to aim for cause-and-effect conclusions. ✓ ✓ They both use a repeated measures design too (they use the same participants for all conditions), which means they both control for participant variables, which is useful when aiming for cause-and-effect conclusions. ✓ Both studies ask their participants to recognise words from a list, which makes them similar, which is not surprising as they both look at cognitive processes. ✓

ⓔ The first sentence this time gets 2 marks (just) as it says just a little more than the first sentence of the other two answers — also the idea of cause and effect is returned to later in the answer. There is a third mark for the comparison of the designs. There is a further mark for the point about using word lists. More needed to be said for the other 2 marks. Reliability could have been mentioned, as the use of the controls and research method chosen aims for this. Validity could also have been referred to, as neither study is really valid due to the reliance on word lists, which are unnatural tasks.

(2) Describe the procedure of Godden and Baddeley (1975). (4 marks, AO1)

ⓔ This question is only about how the study was carried out, so don't give the aim of the study or the results or conclusions. You need to say enough for 4 marks, and a good way of doing this is to say four things about how the study was carried out.

Student answer

The study involved 18 divers who were on a diving holiday in Scotland and agreed to do the study during the holiday, in various locations according to where the dives were planned. ✓ The study used a repeated measures design, as the divers did all four conditions. The conditions were learning the words and recalling them in the same setting and in different settings, with two settings, so there were four conditions. ✓ The divers either learned the words while diving (20 feet deep) or on the shore (sitting with their gear on), and recalled the words either while diving or on the shore. ✓ There were two conditions where learning and recall were in the same setting, and two where there were different settings for learning and recall. It was hard to control the features of the study except for the words and the setting, as the time of day and place of the dive depended on the holiday and what had been arranged, so some features of the situation were not controlled. ✓

ⓔ There are 4 marks here, and the answer shows that you need to know quite a bit about the studies that you look at in detail. Notice that just saying how many participants there were is not enough for a mark — each mark requires a reasonable amount of information.

(3) Evaluate one study in cognitive psychology other than Godden and Baddeley (1975). Make sure you identify the study in your answer. (4 marks, AO2)

ⓔ This question asks you to give good or bad points about a study. The one covered in this guide is Craik and Tulving, though you may have covered a different one. If you have done a different one, practise answering this question using that study.

Student answer

Craik and Tulving (1975). The study was a laboratory experiment that used different questions to focus on words and then asked for recall/recognition of the words. This is an artificial task and could be said not to be about levels of processing information in general, and so to lack validity. ✓ There was also a lack of ecological validity, in that the study was not in the participants' natural setting, which could have led to results that were not real-life — they might have performed differently rather than as they would in processing in their everyday lives. ✓ The study found that not only was there better recall when semantic processing took place, which was said to be deep processing, but the processing then took longer as well, so it is hard to say whether it is deep processing or length of time processing that leads to the best recall. ✓ As a laboratory experiment, it is replicable because of careful controls such as using a tachistoscope to time how long the words were presented for, so the study can be tested for reliability. ✓

ⓔ This answer is thorough and you might get more than 1 mark for the points that use terms and explain them clearly as well. However, note that for questions asking you to evaluate, in general you will have to say more to get the mark than for questions that ask for description. Whatever the question, ensure you make your point fully and clearly, as the last two answers illustrate well.

Key issue

(l) Discuss one key issue you have studied within the cognitive approach, including describing the issue and explaining it with reference to cognitive psychology. (12 marks, essay)

e The marks here are given in levels from an answer that gives no rewardable material (0 marks) to an answer that is well detailed and well focused on the question, giving both description and evaluation. You should describe the issue for a few marks, so that it is clear which issue you are explaining and why it is an issue. Then you should give research — theories and studies — from cognitive psychology to explain the issue. Evaluation can also gain marks and is useful.

Student answer

Eyewitness testimony is an issue that is studied in depth in the cognitive approach, mainly because studies in the approach first highlighted that such testimony might be unreliable. Where someone is convicted of something criminal solely because of eyewitness testimony, there have been many instances of that person being freed on appeal because of understood problems with such testimony. ✓ **AOl** This strongly suggests that there are still people wrongly imprisoned because of eyewitness testimony. It is not suggested that eyewitnesses lie, though that might occur, but that testimony is not as solid as juries and members of the public believe. ✓ **AOl** Elizabeth Loftus carried out many experiments to look at the effect of leading questions on recall, including one study asking about broken glass when there was 'a' broken headlight or 'the' broken headlight. Witnesses seem to take up the suggestion that 'the' broken headlight meant glass, whereas 'a' broken headlight did not suggest glass as strongly. ✓ **AO2** In another study Loftus (with Palmer) showed that changing the verb in a question affected the estimates of the speed of a car in an accident. If cars 'smashed' into one another, a witness estimated a higher speed for the car than if cars 'hit' one another. ✓ **AO2** These two studies suggest that the way a witness is questioned will affect their testimony, which shows that eyewitness testimony is not like a tape recording and can be unreliable. ✓ **AO2** Other factors affecting eyewitness testimony, apart from how questions are asked, include how long after the event the witness is questioned and whether the witness is asked in the same context as that in which the incident occurred. ✓ **AOl** Loftus found, however, that eyewitnesses can be swayed, for example, by how questions are asked or what questions are asked, if the information they are recalling is not central to the situation. Where information was central, witnesses were more sure. ✓ **AOl or AO2** She carried out experiments, which means they were artificial — for example, when asking about the speed of cars after a car accident she showed participants a film. In a real-life accident a witness would be more emotional and that might affect their memory — so her study was not valid. ✓ **AO2** Also, when eyewitness testimony is being studied, the situations that a participant is put into, such as thinking about car accidents, can be stressful, and ethical guidelines suggest that participants are not supposed to be distressed. ✓ **AO2**

ⓔ This answer is not marked point by point, but where a relevant point is made, there is a tick to help you to see how to make relevant points. There is a balance of AO1 and AO2 marks, which is good in this sort of essay, and there is good use of terminology, with clear communication. Giving details about some of the cases where eyewitness testimony has led to a conviction that has subsequently been quashed because of over-reliance on eyewitness testimony would be useful, to add depth to the essay. This essay is likely to be in the band just below the top band, though with a bit more detail it would be a top-band essay. You would expect to get around 9 of the 12 marks for this essay.

Practical

Within cognitive psychology you will have carried out an experiment on some aspect of either memory or forgetting.

(1) (a) Give the aim of your study. (1 mark, AO3)

ⓔ The study on which we focus here for answers is a version of the Craik and Tulving study. You should answer this section using the practical you did for your own course.

Student answer

The aim was to see if semantic processing led to the best recall compared to structural or phonemic processing. ✓

ⓔ This is fine and clear.

(b) Explain one control that you put into place, other than sampling or standardised instructions. (2 marks, AO3)

ⓔ There are situational and participant variables that need to be controlled in an experiment, and the four studies in your course in cognitive psychology are experiments. Sampling and standardised instructions control participant variables, so consider another participant variable or a situational variable for your own study.

Student answer 1

The situation was controlled.

ⓔ This is not enough for a mark, as you must be specific.

Student answer 2

One control is that the questions used to gather the data are the same for everyone, including being typed the same, ✓ using the same word lists for recognition and asking the same questions. ✓

ⓔ This is fine for the 2 marks, as making the apparatus the same is a necessary control and enough is said for 2 marks.

(c) Explain how you gave (or could have given) your participants the right to withdraw.   (3 marks, AO3)

ⓔ There are 3 marks for explaining how the right to withdraw was given. This means that good detail is required.

Student answer

Standardised instructions were read out to participants just before they started to complete the questionnaire, which had the list of questions to gather the data. The instructions thanked everyone in advance for their cooperation and informed them clearly that, at that point, they could withdraw from the study. ✓ The instructions went on to say that each participant could withdraw from the study at any time and would be able to withdraw their data at the end if they wished to. ✓ At the end of the study the participants were thanked again and asked again if their data could be used, and they were reminded that they could withdraw their data if they wished. ✓ Nobody did and all seemed happy to have taken part.

ⓔ This gets the full 3 marks because there is quite a bit of depth. Note that you have to make your points clearly to get the marks.

(d) What was the independent variable and how did you operationalise it?   (4 marks, AO3)

ⓔ The IV is usually fully operationalised but you could give a general IV for this answer first, as you then have to show how it is operationalised anyway. The IV might not get a mark until it is operationalised when given as an answer to another question, but as there are 4 marks here for the IV, detail is needed.

Student answer

The IV was whether structural, phonemic or semantic processing was taking place, ✓ and this was operationalised based largely on Craik and Tulving. Structural processing involved answering whether a word was in capital letters or lower case. ✓ Phonemic processing involved answering whether a word rhymed with another word or not. ✓ Semantic processing involved answering whether a word fitted into a particular sentence or not. ✓

ⓔ This answer gets all 4 marks, but Craik and Tulving is useful for this sort of question as there are three conditions. Where there is only one condition, it will be harder to get full marks for this question. You could justify why the operationalising had taken place.

Knowledge check answers

1 Social psychology involves the study of interactions between people and of group behaviour. It concerns how people live together and the processes involved, such as obedience to those in authority or issues around prejudice and discrimination (for example, looking at why rival football fans can react violently towards one another).

2 For example: the agentic state is when someone obeys a figure of authority as if he or she is acting for them rather than under his or her own volition and decision making. This is not conforming when agreeing — it is following orders, and it can mean going against one's own principles. An example would be a driver taking an alternative route when a policeman stops him continuing on the road he is on and redirects him.

3 Example: reliability and validity. 1) Reliability is getting the same results when doing a study again — the findings can be relied upon because they were not found only once. Validity is also about having findings that can be 'believed' but is different because it means that what is measured in a study represents *real* life in some way. 2) Laboratory experiments with strict controls can be tested for reliability because they can be repeated successfully. However, it is often hard to say that a lab experiment is valid because the controls mean that what is measured may be too artificial.

4 The aim is to see if there are gender differences in in-group favouritism. The IV is whether the participant is male or female. The DV is how many points are given.

5 An independent variable is likely to involve something about each individual such as their age, gender, type of job, groups they belong to, educational background and so on. This is personal data about them. For example, if you measure someone's hostility to see if it is different towards someone of a group to which they do not belong, you need to know about their group membership. Questionnaires often have quite broad aims and the researcher needs a fair amount of personal data to enable him or her to look for patterns.

6 Open questions allow a free response, so the respondent can explain the answer more fully and use their own words. This means an answer to an open question is more likely to be valid in the sense of 'about the respondent's real feelings or behaviour'. Closed questions restrict the response so that answers can be more easily categorised and measured. This means that answers to closed questions are more likely to be found again if asked again, and that the questionnaire is more easily repeated in different circumstances, so the data can be tested for reliability.

7 Qualitative data give rich detail and a lot more information than quantitative data. This means that data are more valid, in that the respondent has the opportunity to interpret a question or statement in their own way rather than to be constrained into answering in the way a researcher suggests. Quantitative data are not as rich or detailed because they often involve ticking 'yes' or 'no' or rating statements. No matter how much better quantitative data are to analyse (such as yielding percentages for comparisons), qualitative data have more value in that they are about real-life situations and attitudes.

8 Descriptive statistics summarise numbers. The mode, median and mean, as well as graphs and charts, all require numbers. Qualitative data are in the form of words and need a different type of analysis. For example, someone's attitudes to people in different groups could range from interested and supportive to hostile and aggressive, and none of these comments could be summarised using numbers. Qualitative data can be grouped into categories and then would become quantitative data if numbers in categories became the data, but in their raw form qualitative data are not suitable for statistical analysis.

9 Questionnaires ask people for their own opinions and feelings — this is about self-report data, as the participants are reporting about themselves. People can say they would do something, such as help someone else, or say they would not do something, such as give what they think is an electric shock to someone else. However, it cannot be known whether they would actually do what they say they would do. In many ways, none of us can know what we would do in a certain situation until it arose. Therefore, questionnaires do not measure actual behaviour. Attitudes may not reflect behaviour.

10 Random sampling means everyone in the chosen population has an equal chance of being chosen. Stratified sampling means choosing people from categories that suit the study so that a certain number from each category is going to be in the sample. Volunteer/self-selected sampling means people put themselves forward as participants. Opportunity sampling means the researcher takes who is available at the time.

11 Questionnaires have generalisability if the sample is large enough and carefully enough chosen, such as using random sampling taken from a sampling frame that represents the target population (or, better still, taken from the whole of the target population). If, however, as often happens with questionnaires, they are posted out and participants are volunteers who return them, then generalisability is in question because volunteers are self-selected and tend to be a particular type of person.

12 Example: informed consent and right to withdraw. Informed consent means that the participant must know what the study is about and what they have to do before they agree to take part, and they must give that informed agreement before the start of the study. Even though they have given informed consent and been deceived as little as possible, throughout the study they must be given the right to withdraw and the offer must be repeated explicitly and often. It is also important that they are given the right to withdraw in such a way that they feel able to withdraw, and this includes withdrawing their data after the study has ended.

13 In a postal questionnaire, the participant just has the written instructions and questions in front of them rather than an individual. In an interview, there is the interviewer. The way they dress and their body language can give clues that lead to demand characteristics and that can lead to bias. The interviewer is likely to be writing down answers perhaps, and can change the answer by using notes — not necessarily deliberately but by summarising. The interview might be taped and that can affect replies given too if the interviewee wants to be seen in a good light (social desirability) or not to say anything that can be used against them (it being taped, there will be evidence).

14 There are structured, unstructured and semi-structured interviews. Structured interviews are good because answers from one respondent can be compared with those from another as they are asked the same things — this is likely to lead to reliability. Unstructured interviews are good because the interviewer can go with the respondent's answers and follow threads that would not be available in a structured interview, which means data are more rich and valid. Semi-structured interviews have the advantage of reliability (given the structured part) and validity (given the unstructured part), and are likely to gather both quantitative and qualitative data.

15 a) Milgram used careful controls with what the participants were told, such as the verbal prods being written out and the instructions being the same for all participants. b) Milgram took care with ethics to the extent of asking colleagues if they thought participants would 'shock' the 'victim' and following up on the participants later, including full debrief. c) Milgram controlled the environment as well as the instructions, having identical equipment for all participants in the same setting and with the same personnel present.

16 a) A strength is the evidence from variations — the less they were agents, the less participants obeyed. b) A weakness is that there are other explanations, such as social power theory — Milgram had expert power and legitimate power. c) A strength is the power of the explanation in real-life situations. The idea can be used to account for acts carried out by people (such as in the Holocaust) that are hard to understand. d) A weakness is the lack of depth in the explanation: obedience is being the agent of an authority figure, because of being their agent — this is tautological.

17 Overall, a surprising 91.7% of those who were in the experimental group gave all the stress remarks and 'punished' the participant, with 73% of the participants being taken in by the experiment and thinking it was about the job application, though participants attributed to the experimenter 45% of the blame for the harm done to the applicant.

18 Example: similarities. a) **Deceit**. Meeus and Raaijmakers used it less because they explained the study more than Milgram did, but both studies deceived the participants. The Dutch study pretended that the job application was real and Milgram pretended that the shocks were real, for example. b) **Right to withdraw**. They were also very similar as both used scripted verbal prods to encourage participants to continue if they showed signs of wanting to stop the study, which is not giving full right to withdraw.

19 Prejudice is attitude about people focusing on some characteristic and it can be positive or negative. Discrimination is acting on that attitude — it is an actual action rather than a feeling, emotion or thought.

20 A football team is likely to see themselves as an in-group and an opposing side as the out-group, which is social identification. They will categorise themselves as an in-group, including wearing their team colours and adopting their team approach, which is social categorisation. Then they will compare their team with an opposing team, seeing the other team as 'bad' and themselves as 'better', which is social comparison. Seeing themselves as better and feeling hostility (prejudice) to the out-group enhances the self-esteem of members, which helps to keep them together as an in-group.

21 **Results**: a) 21 out of 22 nurses went to obey the doctor and 'give' the drug. b) 11 of the 22 said they had not noticed the dosage discrepancy. c) 10 of the 12 graduate nurses asked said that they would not have given the medication (they would not have obeyed the order). **Conclusions**: a) Where there could be two trained 'intelligences' in the care of a patient (doctor and nurse), there was only one in reality (the nurse obeys the doctor), which means less good quality care possibly. b) Nurses will obey a doctor authority figure and do what they are told (presumably in an agentic state). c) Nurses in the field experiment obeyed even though those surveyed said they would not. We do not always do what we think we will do perhaps.

22 a) They wanted to get valid data so wanted to set up a realistic scenario such as one set of the participants really being guards over the other set. b) They wanted to investigate tyranny, which is when one group uses their power against another group. c) They wanted to see if when people can cross between groups there is less in-group/out-group hostility than when they cannot change groups.

23 **Experiment**: a) They manipulated variables such as at first the groups were permeable (people could be swapped between the groups) and later they were not. b) There were controls such as how the participants were selected for each group. **Case study**: a) The setting was a mock prison set up to be natural in the sense of mimicking real life carefully, and then the study looked at 'one prison' using different methods of gathering and recording data, as does a case study. b) There was a small overall group that did not change (except with some small manipulations, for example one person was introduced into the situation later), which is characteristic of a case study (it looks at an individual or small group in detail).

24 With regard to competence, there were two 'ethics committees' to oversee all the procedures throughout. One committee was set up before the study started (made up of five people), to check on ethics from the start. Two clinical psychologists were there to consult and observe. One participant was given the right to withdraw. Informed consent was gained because participants were told all about the study beforehand and they were screened too, to ensure suitability for the study.

25 US soldiers in Iraq were controlling Iraqi prisoners of war in the Abu Ghraib prison. In 2004, it was reported in newspapers that the soldiers had been acting brutally towards the prisoners and pictures showed the horrific nature of the soldiers' acts.

The soldiers were assumed not to be evil as individuals. It was wondered why what appeared to be 'normal' people had done (or were doing) such terrible acts against other human beings. Members of the public wanted answers and there were calls for punishment for such acts.

26 Example: I used opportunity sampling because I used the sixth form students who were in the common room at the time I wanted to do my study and I gave all of them my questionnaire to complete. I gave them the right to withdraw by writing on the top of each questionnaire that they did not have to complete it, could miss questions out and could leave the study at any time.

27 Information processing is part of cognitive psychology and suggests that there is a process (or set of processes) that takes information from the senses and enables us to produce an output from such information. The brain processes information by perception, using features such as eyes and ears to input the information, and the brain to record such information. Selective attention is paid to certain features from sense data and memory processes sort information that is attended to. There are ways of forgetting too, that come from the processing involved. There are similarities between the way the brain processes information and the way a computer processes information.

28 Noise can be a situational variable because noise in the setting of a study can distract participants or noise can be greater for one condition than the other so can affect results. Hunger is a participant variable. One group may do the study just after lunch and the other just before lunch and such differences can affect performance.

29 **Differences**: a) A field experiment is done in surroundings that are natural for the participants, whereas a laboratory experiment is done in an artificial setting. b) In a field experiment, it is hard to control for extraneous variables because the natural setting implies variables that are not controllable, such as traffic noise or temperature. However, in a laboratory setting, variables are a lot more controllable.
Similarities: a) In both a field and a laboratory experiment, there is an IV involving conditions that are manipulated by the researcher. b) In both a field and a laboratory experiment, planning is such that cause-and-effect conclusions are aimed for, so controls are as tight as they can be so that the IV manipulation can be said to *cause* the DV.

30 a) The natural experiment has a naturally occurring independent variable so there is validity in the task and the construct. For example, if a town is measured before and after television is introduced, then conclusions are drawn about the effects of television; there is validity in this. b) The experiment is done in a natural setting, so there is ecological validity as well — it will be 'in the field'.

31 a) Independent groups can be useful as the participant does not have to do more than one condition so will not learn and get better, for example (or get bored). This would be good for two lists of words, with a different condition each, as then the words could be the same. b) Repeated measures can be useful

as it takes away participant differences, so it would work well when learning words underwater and on land. c) A matched pairs design can be good when the conditions need different people (such as when needing to use the same word list) and can also take away participant differences. In a study where one condition was learning in a quiet room and one was learning in a noisy room, the same materials could be used.

32 Participants who learn 20 words underwater will recall more words later when underwater than when recalling the words later on land.

33 Two ways of avoiding order effects include counterbalancing (the order of presentation of conditions is alternated) and randomising the order of conditions (e.g. a coin is tossed each time). A third way, though it may not be practicable, is to use an independent groups design: there will not be order effects as different people do each condition so will not get tired (fatigue effect) or get better at the task (practice effect).

34 Godden and Baddeley carried out a study, they did not suggest a theory, so it would not be right to describe their study in a question about a theory of forgetting. A right answer could be to describe the theory of cue dependency.

35 The least useful for memory is structural processing (what things look like), the next best is phonemic processing (what things sound like) and the best recall is when semantic processing takes place. Semantic processing means attending to meaning.

36 Experiments are strongly controlled so that it can be claimed that the IV causes the change in DV, whereas other methods might not be able to claim a cause and effect relationship so clearly. Experiments have standardised procedures so are quite easily replicable. If studies can be redone and the same results found, the findings are reliable. Other methods tend not to be so standardised so not so easy to repeat. Experiments can take a specific part of the theory, operationalise the variables and then test that specific part, whereas other methods may not be able to operationalise as clearly, and therefore not have such credible findings.

37 This will depend on your own situation. I am typing using a keyboard and looking at a computer screen so they are context dependent cues I might need for later recall. A state dependent cue might be that I am sleepy.

38 The cognitive environment includes the outside environment and the inside one at the time a memory was encoded. If someone forgets something, it can help them to remember (forgetting is less) if the environment is recreated — not just the external environment (where they were and so on) but also the internal environment (what they were thinking, how they felt, what was going on for them mentally at the time). If forgetting is down to not having the retrieval cues, then putting back the retrieval cues can stop the forgetting (help remembering).

39 Example of a strength: there is evidence to support the theory. For instance, Jenkins and Dallenbach as far back as 1924 found that, when given ten nonsense syllables, people who went about their daily business remembered fewer of them than people

who then slept (overnight). They concluded that events during the day interfered with the recall, whereas sleeping meant no interference. Also, Gunter et al. (1980) found that when people watched a number of news items, responses were affected by the older news items, suggesting that old learning interferes with new learning. This supports the idea of proactive interference.

40 They studied in the 'field' of the divers, so it is a field study. However, they also used controls with specific IV and DV, using an experimental method, so it is an experiment. This is a *field experiment*.

41 They use an experimental design (repeated measures) and this means there is control over participant variables. They control the independent variable carefully by setting up four conditions that cover all parts of having learning and recall (two parts) on either land or in the water (two more parts). They keep the syllables of the words used fairly consistent so that there are no longer words to affect recall. Controls such as these, and having a clearly measurable DV as well as a manipulated IV, mean that this research method is experimental.

42 a) Whether the answer was 'yes' or 'no' in their questions for both scenarios, time taken to give the answer rose from structural processing through phonemic processing to semantic processing. b) The proportion of the words recalled when the answer was 'yes' in structural processing was 0.18 compared with 0.96 for semantic processing. c) The proportion of the words recalled when the answer was 'no' in structural

processing was 0.14 compared with 0.83 for semantic processing. d) There is a large difference in proportion of words recalled between structural processing (0.18) and phonemic processing (0.78).

43 Levels of processing theory shows that adding meaning to material means better recall, so summarising to make one's own notes or drawing up diagrams using the material are ways that would need meaning used. Making up acronyms can work too, as that would require deep processing (such as GRAVE for evaluating studies — generalisability, reliability, application, validity, ethics — but making up your own). Cue-dependent forgetting suggests that having cues at storage that can be used for retrieval would also be a good strategy. Imagining the revision session when in the exam, or having actual cues (again perhaps an acronym as a mnemonic), might help.

44 Example: The IV was whether the word required structural processing (whether it was capitals or lower case) or whether it needed semantic processing (did the word fit into the sentence 'fell off the wall'?). The DV was how many of the words were recognised in a list of double the amount of words. One control was that all participants did both conditions and the same materials were used (a questionnaire). The right to withdraw was given at the start, half way through (with a reminder) and at the end (at the debrief, to ask if they were happy for their data to be used).

Glossary

This section contains definitions of the key terms that you need to know for Edexcel AS Psychology Unit 1. They are organised alphabetically and subdivided into each approach.

The social approach

Agency theory Milgram's explanation for obedience to those in authority. He thought that being in an agentic state would benefit society and so might be a behaviour that was handed down through natural selection.

Agentic state the state people are in when they are acting as agents for someone else or society rather than acting according to their own principles and their own decisions.

Alternative hypothesis the statement of what is expected in a study, such as 'young females who have just passed their test are better drivers around a prescribed course than young males who have just passed their test'.

Autonomous state the state people are in when they are acting for themselves and making their own decisions, as opposed to being in an agentic state.

Closed-ended (closed) questions questions that ask for specific responses, where the answers are restrained by boxes or categories of replies such as yes/no answers or ratings on a scale.

Cognitive dissonance a theory put forward by Festinger to account for how people change completely when one aspect of them changes. According to the theory, if someone's behaviour is at odds with their emotions and their thinking, that person experiences feelings of discomfort or guilt; so to resolve these feelings, they have to change their emotions and thinking as well.

Confidence interval the plus or minus figure that shows the extent to which you accept that any results are not likely to be true. For example, you might say you have confidence in the findings of your survey within plus or minus 3 of the percentages found, which is a high confidence level.

Confidence level the percentage of a sample that is likely to represent the population. For example, in a survey you might have a confidence level of 95% because not all the answers will truly represent the population: there are always chance factors for some results, such as a misunderstanding of the question or someone guessing.

Controls procedures in a study that make sure that what is done and measured is not affected by external factors such as noise, time of day, temperature, bias from the researcher or anything else. If a study is carefully and well controlled then findings are secure — they are about what they say they are about. Controls are put in place to avoid bias.

Data results and findings from studies of any sort. Data are what are gathered from a study and can be either qualitative or quantitative.

Debrief an explanation given at the end of a study to a participant, saying what the study was about, what results were expected and how the results will be used. It gives the participant the chance to ask questions and the right to withdraw their data.

Deindividuation the idea that people can become unidentifiable as individuals in certain situations, such as when wearing a uniform or when in a crowd. People can then act in ways in which they would not normally act because their control over themselves as individuals is to an extent lost.

Demand characteristic a feature of a study that gives a clue about what is intended, so that a participant can either try to help the researcher by doing what they think is wanted or be unhelpful. Either way data are not valid so the study is not a good one. It is a form of bias.

Discrimination an action arising from a prejudiced attitude.

Ethics principles of right and wrong with regard to the actions of others or of societies, and issues concerning right and wrong. There are ethical guidelines for the treatment of both human and animal participants of studies. Researchers need to make sure that studies with human participants do not upset anyone and that everyone is treated fairly and with respect.

Experimental hypothesis the alternative hypothesis for an experiment (i.e. for any other research method it is called the alternative hypothesis). The experimental hypothesis is the statement of what is expected in an experiment, such as 'more words from a list are recalled if they are learnt in categories than if learnt as a random list'.

Hypothesis the statement of what is expected when a test or study is to be carried out. The alternative or experimental hypothesis says what is expected, while the null hypothesis says the opposite — that any results found in a study will not be significant enough to draw conclusions and are likely to be due to chance. Statistical tests look to see if results are significant enough to be unlikely to be due to chance.

Informed consent the agreement of participants to take part in a study on the basis that they know what the study is about, and the principle that they must be given this information before taking part.

In-group the group that someone categorises themselves as belonging to.

Interview a way of collecting data by asking spoken questions. Structured interviews have a set of questions that are stuck to. Semi-structured interviews involve some set questions but some allowance for exploring issues. Unstructured interviews involve an interview schedule or set of questions but then the interviewer can explore different areas that arise according to the respondent's answers.

Interviewee a person being interviewed. The participant in an interview is called the interviewee and the participant in a questionnaire is called the respondent.

Likert scale a rating scale that uses categories for gathering data. There might be five points on a scale, for example: 'strongly agree', 'agree', 'unsure', 'disagree', 'strongly disagree'.

Methodology a set of research methods and everything to do with them.

Natural selection according to evolution theory, the passing on of any tendency that aids survival. If an organism with a particular characteristic survives to reproduce, the genes causing that characteristic are passed on.

Null hypothesis the statement that the difference or relationship predicted to happen in a study will not happen. For example, 'young female drivers who have just passed their test will not be better drivers around a prescribed course than young male drivers'. The null hypothesis acknowledges that there might still be a difference in the driving of the two genders but any difference there is will not be large enough to conclude that the difference in driving is because of the difference in gender. The difference could be due to chance or to another factor not considered. A statistical test looks to see if a difference that is found is likely to be due to chance. If the test shows that the difference is large enough for it to be unlikely to be due to chance, then the null hypothesis (which says there is not a large enough difference) will be rejected and the alternative hypothesis (which says there is a difference) will be accepted.

Obedience obeying someone in authority (an authority figure).

Objectivity not allowing personal views to affect analysis, so that findings are relevant, reliable and valid. Science requires objectivity because if factors about a researcher affect results, then the results cannot be used to build a body of knowledge.

Open-ended (open) questions asking for people's opinions and attitudes in a way that allows them to answer in whatever way they like, without being limited in any way.

Opportunity sampling the researcher takes whoever is available to take part in the study. The sample is sometimes called a grab or convenience sample.

Out-group the other group, when someone categorises themselves as being in the in-group. Those in the in-group become prejudiced and discriminate against the out-group.

Participant the person providing the data in a study — the person taking part. The participant used to be called the 'subject' until it was realised that this made them more like an 'object' than an individual with a part in the study.

Personal data information about respondents such as their age, gender, occupation, whether they have a driving licence — whatever is of interest.

Pilot survey a small-scale practice run of a task or survey to find out any problems and put them right before the real thing.

Placebo something pretending to be a substance such as medication when it is actually something else that is harmless, like glucose. It is given so that participants in a study do not know whether or not they are receiving whatever is the subject of the study — or it is given for safety reasons, so that no harm is done.

Prejudice a negative attitude towards someone or a group that results in stereotyping. Prejudice can be positive but is usually negative. Any negative attitude based on uncertain facts is a prejudiced attitude.

Presumptive consent consent to taking part in a study that is assumed to be given even though the actual participants are not fully informed about it. Other people, not the participants, are fully informed and asked if they would take part in such a study; if they would, it is assumed that the actual participants would not mind either.

Prior consent consent to taking part in a study in cases where participants are asked in general if they would be volunteers for a study without knowing exactly what it is about.

Qualitative data opinions and attitudes that are gathered and analysed rather than set answers. In a questionnaire, qualitative data are gathered by open-ended questions.

Quantitative data data gathered in the form of numbers, such as numbers of yes/no answers, and measurable categories, such as ratings on a scale of 0 to 10. In a questionnaire, quantitative data are gathered by closed-ended questions.

Reliability The extent to which the same (or very similar) data are yielded when a test or study is run again. If data from a repeat of the study are very similar, then the study is said to give reliable results. If they were not reliable, findings from the study could not be added to a scientific body of knowledge.

Representative sample a sample in which everyone in the target population is represented. For example, if the target population includes all females, then females of every age should be part of the sample, and perhaps females with different educational backgrounds and different jobs.

Respondent the person giving the answers in a survey; the participant.

Response bias factors in the question or task giving a bias, such as tending to suggest the answer 'yes' and thereafter getting that answer regardless; or bias in the respondent, such as having the type of personality that tends to agree or disagree. Such a person may try to be helpful, for example, and say what they think is wanted.

Response set getting into the habit of answering in a particular way (such as 'yes') to a set of questions and so continuing in that way regardless. This can happen if a Likert-type scale is used and all the statements are phrased so that 'strongly agree' is in the same direction (such as being prejudiced). Such statements should be mixed so that sometimes a prejudiced person would answer 'strongly disagree'. A particular type of response bias.

Sampling the way people are chosen to take part in a study. Usually not all the people being studied can be involved, so there has to be a sample.

Sampling frame the people chosen from among whom the sampling is done. The whole target population cannot usually be chosen, so there is a suitable sampling frame, such as one primary school to represent all primary schools.

Schedule in an interview, the list of questions, any instructions, and any other information such as the length of time for the interview.

Science building a body of knowledge in such a way that others can rely on the knowledge. This involves objectivity, measurable concepts (so that the tests can be done again), careful controls and the generating of hypotheses from previous theory (so that one piece of evidence can link to another one to build the knowledge).

Self-rating giving a rating score about oneself, such as for attractiveness or meanness.

Simple random sampling a method of sampling by which everyone in the sampling frame or target population has an equal chance of being chosen to be included in the sample.

Social categorisation a process of accepting oneself as being part of an in-group, according to social identity theory.

Social comparison the process of comparing one's in-group with the out-group and thinking of the in-group as better in some way. This enhances the individual's self-esteem and can lead to prejudice.

Social desirability the tendency we have to say what we think we ought to say or do what we ought to do in a given situation. For example, it is socially desirable to say we recycle rubbish, so a survey is likely to find that we do — even if we do not — because we are likely to say that we do. It is a form of bias.

Social identification a process of identifying with an in-group after categorising oneself as being part of the in-group.

Stereotyping transferring an opinion about an individual onto other individuals or groups.

Stratified sampling a method of sampling by which the target population is divided into required groups or strata, and corresponding proportions of people from these groups are picked out for the sample.

Subjectivity allowing personal views to affect analysis so that findings are affected.

Surveys interviews and questionnaires in which questions are asked to gather data.

Target population all the people the results will be applied to when the study is done.

Validity the extent to which a test or study yields data that apply to a real-life setting and real-life situations; the extent to which the data are 'true'. If a study is measuring what it claims to measure (for example, if it has really found out about prejudice and not just what we think we should say about prejudice) then it is said to give valid results. If they were not valid, findings from the study could not be added to a scientific body of knowledge.

Volunteer/self-selected sampling a method of sampling by which people are asked to volunteer for the study, either personally or via an advertisement. They self-select themselves by volunteering.

The cognitive approach

Baseline measure a measure of what would 'normally' be the case, so that in an experiment a difference can be tested for. It comes from the control group; the researcher compares the control group with the experimental group to see what difference the experiment has made.

Capacity size; in the multi-store model of memory, the size of a store and the storage space available.

Central executive according to the working-memory model, it is the controller of the system. It controls the flow of information and the processing; for example, it gets information into one stream and controls whether the phonological loop or visuospatial scratchpad is needed.

Cognitive environment is the physical environment, emotional state and thinking state when encoding takes place and gives retrieval cues that activate a memory trace.

Computer analogy the idea that the brain can be likened to a computer, with input (from the senses), throughput (the processing) and output.

Conditions parts or aspects of the independent variable, such as whether words are in capitals (visual), whether they rhyme (auditory) or whether they fit into a sentence correctly (semantic).

Confabulation making up bits of an event when retelling it so that it makes more sense, which means a memory is not exactly like the perception of the event.

Confounding variables extraneous variables that seem to have affected the results of a study. For example, in a study memory was found to be better when recall was in the same context as learning; but in practice it was found that all those studied in the same context were younger than those studied in a different context, so age would be a confounding variable.

Context-dependent forgetting forgetting that occurs when the cues that were in the environment at encoding are missing at recall (leading to forgetting). There are cues about the situation and the context. This is as opposed to state-dependent forgetting.

Control group the group in an experiment that is producing a baseline measure of what would 'normally' happen without the manipulated condition in the experiment, such as learning a random list of letters rather than a grouped list and trying to recall them.

Counterbalancing alternating the conditions for each participant in an experiment to help to control for order effects in a repeated measures design. If there are two conditions, for example, the first participant does condition one followed by condition two. Then the second participant does condition two followed by condition one and so on.

Cue-dependent forgetting forgetting that occurs because of the lack of a retrieval cue in the cognitive environment at the time of retrieval so a memory trace is not activated.

Demand characteristics characteristics found when a participant's responses are affected by them guessing what the study is about.

Dependent variable (DV) what is being measured as a result of the experiment and as a result of the independent variable being manipulated. For example, when doing an experiment looking at the effect of interference on short-term memory in the number of letters recalled, the dependent variable of the study would be how many letters are recalled.

Directional hypothesis a hypothesis that predicts the direction of the results, such as whether more or fewer words are recalled. For example, 'recall of letters is greater if letters are grouped (chunked) than if they are not'.

Double-blind technique a procedure where neither the participants nor the person doing a study are aware of what is expected. It is used so that the experimenter cannot affect the results of the study because of their expectations.

Dual-task paradigm an experimental technique that involves two tasks, sometimes using the same systems and sometimes not, to see what those systems are and how they work. For example, there can be two visual tasks which the person will find hard, or a visual task and an auditory one, which they will find less hard. It was used by Baddeley and Hitch to test their working-memory model.

Duration the time something lasts. In the multi-store model it refers to how long a memory can stay in a store until it is lost (or the trace decays).

Ecological validity the extent to which the setting of a study is real-life. If the setting is a natural one, then the study has ecological validity and in that sense the findings are about real life. However, if the setting is not natural, as in a laboratory experiment, then the study lacks ecological validity, and the findings might not be about real life.

Encoding the first part of memory. Material has to be taken into the brain and held there somehow. Information comes from sense data and encoding can be visual, auditory or semantic — and perhaps in other forms such as touch. Encoding is about registering the information.

Engram the structural change in the brain that is a memory.

Experimental group the group in an experiment which is doing the condition that is of interest, such as learning grouped letters and then trying to recall them rather than a randomised list.

Experimenter effects features of the researcher that affect the results of a study, such as tone of voice or facial expression. These might lead the participant to react in certain ways.

Extraneous variables things that might affect the results of a study instead of or as well as the independent variable, such as noise, heat, light or some characteristic of the participants.

Fatigue effect an order effect that occurs when the first part or condition of a study is done better than a later one because the participant is tired by the time they do the second condition.

Field experiment an experiment with as many controls as possible and a manipulated independent variable, but conducted in the field rather than in a lab situation. In the field means in the participant's natural setting.

Forgetting not being able to recall something that could be recalled earlier. Forgetting is probably not one thing at all but a term for different ways of not remembering, including repression (which is motivated forgetting) and displacement (which is when new memories push old ones out).

Incidental learning learning that occurs when participants (or anyone) learn something without deliberately focusing on it, which would be intentional learning.

Independent variable (IV) what is being manipulated by the researcher. This is what is of interest in the study, and what is being tested. For example, when doing an experiment looking at the effect of interference on short-term memory in the number of letters recalled, the independent variable would be whether there is interference in the task or not.

Information processing the way that information comes into the brain via the senses, has something done to it (i.e. it is processed) and then is output in some form. There is a flow of information into, through and out of the brain. This is what the cognitive approach is all about.

Intentional learning learning something by focusing on it and using strategies.

Intersection the crossing of searches in the spreading-activation model. A search from one starting node crosses with a search from another starting node.

Interval/ratio a level of measurement where data are real measurements such as time or temperature. A mean average is suitable.

Laboratory experiment an experiment in a controlled setting that is also artificial, i.e. not in the participant's natural environment. In a lab experiment, there is often an experimental group and a control group, standardised instructions and good control over all variables other than the independent variable.

Levels of measurement ways in which data are scored or measured. There are three main levels of measurement for psychology at AS and A2: nominal, ordinal and interval/ratio.

Levels of processing framework the model of memory that says that the more semantic the processing, including elaboration and depth, the better the recall or recognition. Semantic means adding/using meaning while processing.

Lexical network the dictionary where words are kept (according to their sound, not their meaning), according to the spreading-activation model of memory.

Long-term memory the third store for memory, according to the multi-store model. Information that is rehearsed passes from the short-term memory to the long-term memory.

Mean a measure of central tendency (average) that is calculated by totalling the scores and then dividing by how many scores there are. It is only useful for data at the interval/ratio level of measurement.

Measures of central tendency averages, which include the mode, median and mean.

Measures of dispersion measures of how the data are spread around the mean. The range is a measure of dispersion, as is the standard deviation.

Median a measure of central tendency (average) that is worked out by finding the middle score. If there is no middle score the median is mid-way between the two either side of the middle. For example, out of ten scores the median is between the fifth and sixth score.

Memory encoding, storage and retrieval of experience. Without remembering, a person cannot function. There are different theories of memory, such as that it involves different levels of processing. Another theory suggests there is short-term and long-term memory.

Memory trace a piece of information laid down and retained as a result of the perception of an event.

Modality-specific when information is stored in the same form in which it is received. Information from the eyes is stored as an image, and from the ears is stored as sound.

Mode a measure of central tendency (average) that is worked out by finding the most common score. If there is more than one 'most common' score, then all are given. For example, if there are two modal scores, the data set is bi-modal.

Mode of representation the way memories are stored and the format they are stored in. A mode of representation or type of storage could, for example, be visual or semantic.

Natural experiment an experiment that is usually in the field rather than in a lab because it involves finding a naturally occurring independent variable. For example, natural experiments have been done to look at the effects of television on children (such as aggression) when they can be measured before television is introduced in the area and then measured afterwards to see if there are effects. The researchers do not themselves make children have no television and then have television because that would not be ethical (or practical).

Node a concept or word that is part of the semantic network, according to the spreading-activation model.

Nominal a level of measurement that means data are in categories only, with no numbers assigned. If data include whether someone is aggressive or not, that is nominal data. Measures of central tendency are not useful here.

Non-directional hypothesis a hypothesis in which no direction is predicted and the results can be either 'more' or 'less'. For example, 'recall of letters is affected by whether or not letters are grouped (chunked)'.

Null hypothesis the statement that any difference or relationship predicted in a study will be due to chance (in other words there is no relationship or difference as predicted). It is the hypothesis that is tested when using statistical tests.

Operationalise to make a variable measurable. If you wanted to test helpfulness it would be difficult to know where to start, but you could operationalise helpfulness by measuring whether someone asking for directions was shown the way or not.

Order effects effects that occur when the order of conditions in a study (in a repeated measures design) affects the responses of the participant. They include fatigue and practice effects.

Ordinal a level of measurement that means data are ranked so that the smallest score has rank 1 and so on. The mode and median are suitable averages to use.

Paired associate learning giving participants two words to learn as a pair and then testing them by giving them one of the words (usually the left-hand word in the pair) and asking for recall of the other word.

Parallel processing more than one operation or processing taking place in the brain at the same time.

Participant variables variables such as age, gender, experience and mood.

Phonological loop according to the working-memory model, it deals with sound information. There is an articulatory loop where rehearsal takes place too. The phonological loop has been called the 'inner ear' and the articulatory loop has been called the 'inner voice'. This helps to explain what they are for.

Practice effect an order effect that occurs when the second part or condition of a study is done better than the first because participants are practised by the time they do the second condition.

Primary memory refers to Type I processing, where information at one level is recycled at that level by repetition. For example, auditory information is 'heard' again. Type II processing involves adding something such as meaning.

Priming activating nodes and links ready for understanding and memory. For example, priming 'red' will activate relevant nodes such as other colours, fire, apple, cherries and roses.

Proactive interference the interference of something learned earlier with current learning. For example, learning Spanish first and French next means difficulty in learning the French.

Randomisation making the order in which the participant does the conditions random, to control for order effects in a repeated measures design. If a study has two conditions, for example, there can be a toss of the coin to see which condition the participant will do first.

Range a measure of dispersion. The range is calculated by taking the lowest score from the highest score. Sometimes you have to take 1 away from that calculation to get the range.

Rationalisation shortening a story to make it make sense. This shows that memory is reconstructive, as Bartlett claimed.

Replicability the extent to which a study is easy to repeat or replicate. A study is replicable if there are careful controls and if there is enough detail about the procedure to do the study again.

Retrieval getting to the memories stored in the brain. A problem with retrieval will lead to forgetting. One theory suggests that retrieval can be aided by cues.

Retrieval cue something in the person's cognitive environment at the time of retrieval that activates a memory trace.

Retroactive interference when something learned later gets in the way of something learned before. For example, learning Spanish first and French next means difficulty remembering the Spanish.

Schemata pre-existing ideas that have been built through experience and are plans for what we think will happen and what we know. For example, we might have a schema (the singular of schemata) for 'baking baked potatoes' or one for 'going on holiday on a train'. Our ideas affect how we remember events.

Semantic refers to the meaning of something. Semantic encoding would be registering the information in the form of its meaning, as you might with a word.

Semantic network part of the spreading-activation model of memory; it is the network of linked nodes, which contain concepts and ideas.

Sensory register the first store for memory, according to the multi-store model, where information comes into the brain from the senses. Information lasts less than a second and if it is attended to, it goes to the short-term store. If it is not attended to, it is then not available. Information is stored in the same form as it is received, so is modality-specific. Information from the eyes is stored as an image, and from the ears is stored as sound.

Serial processing performing one operation or process at a time.

Short-term memory the second store for memory, according to the multi-store model. Information that is attended to in the sensory register passes to the short-term memory; if it is then rehearsed, it gets to the long-term memory.

Single blind technique used in a study to avoid expectations of participants affecting results and means the participants are not aware of which group they are in or what results are expected.

Situational variables variables to do with the situation, such as temperature, noise, interruptions and light.

Standard deviation a measure of dispersion that you can learn about for your course, but you do not have to. The standard deviation is worked out by taking all the scores away from the mean average to see how far the scores fluctuate around the mean. Whether they fluctuate or not can show how far they are spread around the mean average, which helps when interpreting the data.

Standardised instructions written sets of instructions to the participants in a study so that all participants get the same information and are not biased by being told something different.

State-dependent forgetting forgetting that occurs when the cues that were in the environment at encoding and are missing at recall (leading to forgetting) are cues about the state and mood of the individual. This is as opposed to context-dependent forgetting.

Storage the retention of information ready for retrieval. One type of forgetting is a problem with storage, another type can be a problem with retrieval.

Tachistoscope a box where the participant looks through a screen and can see letters, words or whatever is of interest flash up for a very short time at the back of the box. The researcher can control the time the stimulus is exposed for and the time between exposures.

Theory an idea about why an event happens, usually based on previous theories and research.

Threshold firing in the brain does not have to be all or nothing (there is a signal or there is not), but there has to be a level of activity (or threshold) before a signal is triggered. Firing in the brain does not have to mean sending a signal, and not firing does not have to mean there isn't a signal. It is likely that there is a threshold of activity before which there is no signal and after which there is a firing of the signal. A set amount of activity is required rather than just 'off' or 'on'.

Variables whatever influences are likely to affect an experiment, including what is being tested, what is being measured and anything else likely to affect the results. They include confounding variables, extraneous variables, the independent variable and the dependent variable. There are also situational variables and participant variables.

Visuospatial scratchpad according to the working-memory model, it deals with visual information. The scratchpad holds spatial information and information about images. The scratchpad could be called the 'inner eye'.

Note: **bold** page numbers refer to key terms.